Free from Addiction

Facing Yourself and Embracing Recovery

Morteza Khaleghi, Ph.D.
with
Constance Loizos

palgrave
macmillan

FREE FROM ADDICTION
Copyright © Morteza Khaleghi, Ph.D., 2008.

First published in 2008 by
PALGRAVE MACMILLAN®
in the United States—a division of St. Martin's Press LLC,
175 Fifth Avenue, New York, NY 10010.

Where this book is distributed in the UK, Europe and the rest of the world,
this is by Palgrave Macmillan, a division of Macmillan Publishers Limited,
registered in England, company number 785998, of Houndmills,
Basingstoke, Hampshire RG21 6XS.

Palgrave Macmillan is the global academic imprint of the above companies
and has companies and representatives throughout the world.

Palgrave® and Macmillan® are registered trademarks in the United States,
the United Kingdom, Europe and other countries.

ISBN-13: 978–0–230–60611–1
ISBN-10: 0–230–60611–3

Library of Congress Cataloging-in-Publication Data

Khaleghi, Morteza.
    Free from addiction : facing yourself and embracing recovery / Morteza
Khaleghi with Constance Loizos.
        p. cm.
    Includes bibliographical references and index.
    ISBN 0–230–60611–3
        1. Substance abuse—Popular works. I. Loizos, Constance. II. Title.

RC564.29.K53 2008
362.29—dc22   2008021604

A catalogue record of the book is available from the British Library.

Design by Newgen Imaging Systems (P) Ltd., Chennai, India.

First edition: October 2008

10 9 8 7 6 5 4 3 2 1

Printed in the United States of America.

Contents

Acknowledgments

I WANT TO THANK Constance Loizos for her diligence in research and dedication to learning about dual diagnosis, and for bringing to life the work we do at Creative Care.

And thank you to Helena Echlin for help in organizing this book in its initial phase.

I also want to thank Luba Ostashevsky and everyone at Palgrave Macmillan for their enthusiasm and expertise in bringing this book to print.

Dedication

I DEDICATE THIS BOOK to my wife, Dr. Karen Khaleghi, and to my children Farrah, Seymone, Dustin and Skylar.

And to the staff at Creative Care for their patience and support as we wrote the book. They show the highest professionalism and care to each and every patient—even on the most challenging days. Our success would not have been possible without this extraordinary team.

And to all who are battling or have freed themselves from addiction. This book is written with you in our hearts—in hopes of guiding you toward true freedom.

PART I

Addiction

Introduction

Debunking the Addiction Myth

*I*N MY 25 YEARS of experience in treating patients with chemical dependence on drugs and alcohol, I have come to two crystal-clear conclusions about addiction and its complexities. First is that every single addict can be helped, no matter how far gone they seem to be, no matter how seemingly determined they are to hurt or even to kill themselves. Second is that addiction does not happen in a vacuum, and it does not happen simply because someone has a genetic propensity to become an addict.

Addiction is always—always—associated with underlying emotional issues that help to fuel it.

The spectrum of emotional issues to which I'm referring is as rich as any rainbow you might see. Some are biochemical, some are not.

Some can be vanquished with a little attention; some require inten-sive psychotherapy and even medication. Think depression, bipolar disorder, anxiety. Think bulimia, anorexia. Think posttraumatic stress disorder (PTSD). Think child abuse. Think neglect. Think traumas, both big and small. Think of every addict you've ever known—in your family, or in your circle of friends, or in your office—ask yourself whether you believe those individuals have suffered from the "disease" of alcoholism or drug addiction alone.

I know that addiction and emotional issues go hand in hand because I see it in living color every day of my life. I know it to be true because I have treated hundreds of people whom traditional addiction treatment has failed, often repeatedly. I know it to be true because so many of my patients—dearly loved people whose families were on the painful brink of total despair—do the most surprising thing when treated for both their addictions and their underlying emotional issues: they turn their lives around. I have seen mothers who once locked themselves in their bedrooms for days and drunk themselves into a stupor return to their children. I have seen fathers, once too doped up to make school plays and birthday parties, make their way back home, and I have seen chil-dren in the throes of painful adolescence wrest themselves from the alternate universe of drug use and fill out college applications. I have seen people hell-bent on destroying themselves learn the gift of sobriety and health, and I have watched them get well.

My motivation for writing this book is to help anyone suffering from addiction, as well as their families and loved ones, to better understand the problem.

I want to share why there is every reason to hope for better days and why I have a personal stake in what I am about to tell you.

THE EVOLUTION OF "DR. K"

Growing up, I didn't imagine that I'd become an expert in addiction. Looking back, though, I realize I've been on this path since I was a child in Tehran, Iran, five decades ago.

Mine wasn't an exceptional childhood. I was the youngest of eight children—which is notable today—but I was happy and close to my siblings and parents, thanks in part to a culture that greatly valued the family unit and its togetherness. It really allowed me to experience not only my own growing up but that of my immediate family.

I was a child who was in tune with those around him and aware of relationships between family and friends. Part of what I absorbed was how much my parents loved me, and I very much wanted to please them in turn: my mother because I adored her, and my father because I admired him. He was a self-educated entrepreneur who left school at a young age to make his own way in the world, and through hard work he provided every comfort for his family.

To make them proud, I worked very hard in school. Along the way, my dedication paid off; I always received high marks. As I grew older, I began to understand what my parents had long instilled in all of their children: that good grades could broaden one's options.

It was something my oldest brother, who is 25 years my senior, took to heart. He became an orthopedic surgeon in Iran, where he continues to practice today.

Two of my other brothers, Mustafa and Ahmad, were also ambitious, so they also studied hard, and after they graduated from high school, both went to the United States to pursue undergraduate and then advanced degrees. As the baby of the family, I absolutely worshipped the ground my brothers walked on, and as a young man who was forming ideas about how he would spend the rest of his life, I began to resolve that I, too, would go to college in the United States. I didn't know what I would find, but I knew that with my brothers close by, I could handle anything.

Then, before I left, something happened that changed the world for me: My mother died after a very short, painful battle with stomach cancer. I was 17 years old at the time the cancer was discovered, and I learned of it just two months before she died. My siblings didn't say anything sooner because they wanted to protect me as long as possible from her dreadful prognosis.

I was shocked to find out about her illness, and, left with little time to process this news, I was devastated when she succumbed to the cancer shortly thereafter. Her death left a gaping hole in my life. Being her youngest child my mother was particularly nurturing of me, and I reciprocated with my affections. She was my best friend, my biggest supporter, and her love of her children gave all of us a level of safety and comfort that I would later realize as a special gift that not nearly enough people enjoy.

I was intensely sad after her death. When I left for the States the next year, I knew that my life would be forever changed and that, with my mother no longer alive, it was unlikely that I would return to Iran. I was too young to know then that the sense of loss and abandonment that I experienced around her death would give me a greater understanding and compassion for those who have suffered their own profound losses.

When I arrived in this country, I joined my two older brothers in California. As is the case for many immigrants, the transition to a new country and culture wasn't easy. In fact, my brother Ahmad, who had begun struggling with seemingly inexplicable periods of depression, grew suicidal at one point and returned to

Iran, feeling that it was not possible for him to live happily so far from family and the familiar surroundings of home.

For Gossem, the idea of returning home was very comforting. And I could certainly understand that. I, too, had periods of intense loneliness and self-doubt. I wondered if I was making the right decision, leaving everything I knew and nearly everyone I loved. But I felt too proud to return. And California was compelling: The weather was beautiful, the people were beautiful. And more important, the freedoms and liberties and opportunities that people seemed to enjoy all around me were beautiful. So I resolved to stay. After enrolling in English-as-a-second-language classes and getting a tentative handle on English—the mastery of which continues to be a pursuit of mine—I started classes at Glendale Community College in Southern California.

At first I didn't know what to study. But by my second term, I was completely turned on to psychology, in part thanks to a very encouraging professor. He made me realize that I'd always been fascinated by the field, an interest that really blossomed after I lost my mother—I had been drawn to people who demonstrated emotional difficulties.

What I was too confused at the time to recognize was that this attraction was a way for me unwittingly to work out my own issues, including a fear of abandonment. In fact, I was so blind to the help I needed that it was only when I was in graduate school, when my curriculum called for 50 hours of psychoanalysis over the course of one year, that I finally began to tackle some of my own ghosts.

The work was a revelation—so much so that I wound up seeing a psychoanalyst three times a week for the next 18 years. I was 28 at the time, and I wish I'd begun treatment earlier. I consider those 18 years the best investment in myself that I've ever made.

DISCOVERING A PATH

When I was a young man in Tehran I had no idea what addiction entailed. Many traditional cultures that base their value systems on honor and shame still don't acknowledge addiction. We knew people who drank and smoked hashish and opium but we weren't sensitive to the extent of their use nor how it governed their lives. In fact, I hadn't given the concept of addiction more than a passing thought, and then it was only when I heard of a friend in trouble or saw someone in the streets of Tehran or on the boardwalks of Los Angeles—someone who was obviously under the influence of something that made him bleary-eyed and mean-tempered and seemingly miserable in his own skin. Addiction? As far as I knew, no one in my family was addicted to anything. My father and my mother never drank. In fact, none of my siblings drank either, as it was culturally and religiously forbidden. It was not until my brothers and I went to the United States that we tasted alcohol for the first time.

I was completely mistaken to think we were immune, though. And I would learn just how wrong I was through my brother Mustafa.

I completed graduate school—where, incidentally, I met my wonderful wife, Karen, who is also a psychoanalyst—in the early 1980s and I decided to open my own practice with another doctor whom I knew and respected. There we treated hundreds of patients, all of whom had psychiatric issues, and a smaller percentage of whom also had problems with addiction. That smaller percentage of addicts concerned us, but in our determination to solve our patients' emotional problems, we didn't focus on their addictions. The reason? Like most other psychologists at the time, we didn't view addiction and emotional issues as two sides to the same coin. Our job was to treat our patients' emotional wounds.

What pills they took or what drinks they snuck outside our offices—well, we hardly approved, but we reasoned that we could only do so much. We rationalized that for their addictions, groups like Alcoholics Anonymous could do much more than we were equipped to do.

We weren't alone in this thinking. It was how the world operated at the time. And it's how much of the world continues to operate, with addiction in one camp and emotional issues in another. Mental health professionals believe that drug and alcohol use can hamper the course of therapy, so it's customary for them to refuse to see patients unless they first stop using drugs and alcohol entirely. Even when doctors do treat addicts, many wrongly believe that if they tackle the issues underlying addiction, the habit will clear up all by itself, so they ignore it.

Exacerbating this divide is how our educational institutions work: Mental health professionals seldom have the necessary training to treat both issues. Most doctoral degrees in clinical psychology require only one course in treating addiction. Although many professionals have expertise in identifying, diagnosing, and treating psychiatric disorders, most lack detailed knowledge about the specific drugs that people abuse, the evolution of abuse and addiction, and how to handle addiction treatment, relapse, and recovery. Similarly, most addiction specialists have little training in psychology; they are much more focused on how to retrain the body away from addictive substances.

It pains me to think of the patients I might have helped back then, but I learned of my mistake soon enough, when Mustafa began to suffer from addiction and severe emotional problems—simultaneously. I'd like to say that a light went on in my mind as soon as this happened, that I suddenly realized that the two might be inextricably linked. Unfortunately, I didn't immediately understand that his becoming an alcoholic when he did was no coincidence. By the time I came to discover that addiction and emotional issues are as closely intertwined as the threads in a piece of fabric, it was too late. And the outcome was devastating.

My brother's journey into darkness began sometime in his early 30s, nearly a decade after he graduated from UCLA with a master's degree in engineering. Twelve years my senior, he had always been very popular. He seemed to have it all. Not only was he was very smart—growing up, I turned to him for tutoring on more occasions that I can remember—but he was also handsome and flamboyant, the star of our family. He was cherished by everyone even more than my eldest brother, the surgeon. I still marvel at how easily Mustafa could command love and attention from everyone, including me.

Things started to go wrong when Mustafa became captivated with acting shortly after receiving his master's degree. Once he became committed to any idea, he worked tirelessly toward realizing it. In this case, it meant giving up on engineering, moving to New York from California, and studying acting at the Lee Strasberg Theatre and Film Institute.

Mustafa may not have anticipated the intensity of his studies or the emotional toll it would take on him. Though he didn't discuss it much with anyone, it was clear that while studying acting, Mustafa occasionally sank into periods of depression, then flew into periods of mania. Maybe he wasn't as good as wanted to be. Maybe acting made him more vulnerable. I really don't know. But to deal with his emotional life, my brother, whom to my knowledge had never consumed much alcohol or used drugs, suddenly took up drinking heavily.

He was 33 at the time. At first, he drank only socially. Then, fairly quickly, he began drinking so much that his binges hampered his ability to perform. And that's if he even made it out of his apartment, which became one of the only places where he knew that he could drink himself into a stupor without calling attention to himself. For someone who had always been very self-possessed— or at least, that was the impression he gave, even to his family— his fall from grace was humiliating.

To hear Mustafa tell it, he was supposed to be Strasberg's next protégé. He was supposed to be the next Al Pacino. Still, he continued to sabotage himself, and on one very important occasion, when he was about to perform a role before Strasberg and some other luminaries in the theater community, something terrible happened: Mustafa froze. He forgot his lines. It was as if he were all alone. He just stared into the quiet darkness, sweating under the stage lights. When someone snapped him out of his paralysis by clearing his throat, Mustafa turned and left the stage.

Many people suffer public embarrassments, but this was unbearable for my brother. He knew immediately how disappointed Strasberg would be, and he felt completely devastated. He was so mortified, so disgraced. I think he concluded right then that he would never make it as an actor. He didn't tell me what had happened until weeks after the incident took place, and even then, he couldn't laugh about it or find the silver lining. It still filled him with shame.

Mustafa's state of mind worsened after he became involved with a married woman whose husband lived overseas. She was very young and newly immigrated, and the two lived happily—if wrongly—on her husband's resources for several years. When her husband eventually dissolved the marriage, the new couple was left penniless, and soon afterward, they, too, drifted apart.

Mustafa grew more and more isolated and continued to drink heavily. My family, like most, was unsure of what to do. My father essentially commissioned me to watch him—which proved difficult because I was in California while Mustafa was in New York—and he supported Mustafa financially in the hope that he would regain his footing. But Mustafa's severe depression, along with his sense of failure for not accomplishing what he'd set out to do—succeed in acting—consumed him.

And "consume" is not overstating things. On the contrary, at the age of just 35, my beautiful brother tried to kill himself by cutting his own throat. It was a dramatic cry for help—can you imagine anything more dramatic?—yet we still didn't appreciate the straits he was in; we couldn't figure out how to right the ship, so to speak.

I consulted with my dad, brothers, and a doctor who saw my brother. It was decided that a "tough love" approach would work best. For my part, I let Mustafa know that I loved him but he needed to get his life in order, and he shouldn't expect coddling from me or the rest of our family.

At the time, this tough love philosophy dominated addiction treatment. In fact, it still does, promising reform through confrontation, often in an isolated environment where an addict cannot escape the need to change his or her behavior.

Mustafa was too old to be sent to a military-style boot camp—which is what many tough love proponents advocate is necessary—but if we'd been able to ship him off, we might have done so, because it was commonly held then that ultimatums and constructive coercion were more helpful to addicts than lovingly delivered confrontations. And though I inherently questioned the very notion of making my suffering brother go through more suffering, I accepted that common wisdom, assuming that it was supported by data.

It is a decision I will always regret.

Soon after his first suicide attempt, Mustafa intentionally, and fatally, overdosed on a lethal combination of painkillers—the benzodiazepine Xanax, a short-acting drug used to treat anxiety and severe depression—and alcohol. All that remained was a suicide note, attempting to absolve all of us of any guilt by saying, "It's nobody's fault; I did this on my own." I know this because when he took his own life, I was the one who discovered him.

Only later did I realize that Mustafa had struggled with undiagnosed clinical depression for some time and that depression runs in ripples throughout my family. (Remember, my brother Ahmad experienced suicidal thoughts, as well.)

I'm sure Mustafa never recognized what plagued him. Growing up, my family put him on a pedestal. I think he felt that that there was a great deal of expectation around what he would become. I also think that he pretended to have great confidence when he in fact he did not. And because "depression" wasn't in our family vocabulary—like addiction, it simply wasn't something we were aware of when we were younger—he likely never imagined that the lows he experienced were biochemical. I'm sure he thought he brought them on himself, and he punished himself for them.

It is my brother whom I see before me when I reach out to those who are suffering. It was his suicide that propelled me further into learning and understanding the emotional lives of those who suffer from addiction. After losing Mustafa, I vowed to myself that I would help those who suffered not only from addiction but from emotional pain—what I ultimately realized as two inextricably linked pieces of the same puzzle. The reason: There are many Mustafas out there. And many people turn to alcohol and other substances to cope with much more than depression. They become addicts because of a wide range of emotional issues.

Clinical depression affects between 8 to 17 percent of the U.S. population on at least one occasion before age 40.

Indeed, over the years of our education, my wife, Karen, and I have shared numerous goals, but the most important one has been and remains furthering the understanding and treatment of addicts' emotional lives. I didn't need to explain to her why I wanted to make it my life's work. She understood the pain of my brother all too well; similar circumstances had wrecked her own family. For years, her father was severely depressed—much more so than her family appreciated because he was private about his emotions, as many men are. (That is the reason why many more men than women kill themselves every year.)

She, too, came to understand the ties between addiction and emotions, which is why, after we both received our doctorate degrees, Karen and I worked in various treatment programs, learning all that we could while we planned to open our own program. We wanted to do what no program at the time was even imagining: We wanted to treat addicts for their addictions and the emotional issues that they feed on.

Thankfully, we managed to realize our dreams. In 1989, we opened Creative Care, an addiction treatment practice that now has facilities in both Malibu and Northridge, California. The decision has been among the most rewarding in our lives. Every month we have the opportunity to help dozens of people who are living with both addiction and emotional issues. We treat between 150 to 200 people annually.

Still, the work we do at the treatment center isn't enough. Many more people can benefit from our approach than we can personally impact at Creative Care. That is why I'm writing this book. I want to go a step further. I want to help as many people as possible to understand what our approach entails, who needs it, and why, in an overwhelming number of cases, treating addiction without exploring and addressing the person's interior life is a recipe for failure.

I also want to show there is reason for hope if you or someone you know suffers from addiction and emotional pain. Help is available. In fact, the most important point I hope to convey in this book is that it's important not to get discouraged. Addiction treatment is a process. Anyone who tells you there is an instant fix is lying. Recovery requires hard work on the part of the patient. There will be ups and downs. There will be setbacks and disappointments and even relapses. And yet in the face of overwhelming challenges, you cannot give up, because my experience has shown that anything is possible and to never, ever stop trying to achieve recovery.

Treating addiction while not dealing with the addict's inner life is a recipe for failure.

Redefining Addiction and Our Treatment

W HAT IS ADDICTION? The reference guide of the mental health field, the *Diagnostic and Statistical Manual for Mental Disorders* (*DSM*), defines addiction as "a compulsive behavior that recurs despite harmful consequences to the individual." The *DSM* distinguishes between physical and psychological dependence and suggests separate treatments. According to the *DSM*, people need medication to let go of the chemical reliance on a narcotic—either alcohol or drugs; psychological dependence does not require medication. Yet any psychologist will tell you that when you start to dig into the root causes of addiction, the easy distinctions start to blur. Can physical need alone drive compulsion? When a person develops a physical dependence on narcotics, is it enough to try to undo the psychological attachment?

Based on my 25 years of experience working with addicts, I believe that it is inaccurate to separate chemical and psychological afflictions. My aim in this book is to show that emotional trauma lies at the heart of every addiction. By this I mean that an event (or series of events) occurred that hurt the person to the point where it causes emotional pain years and decades later. The person may not recall the event or be able to acknowledge its role, but it continues to haunt him or her. This trauma keeps addicts from feeling whole without the aid of alcohol, narcotics, or other compulsions, such as eating, shopping, or participating in intense romantic relationships. The emotional void inside them requires constant upkeep. Addiction is strongly associated with the brain's reward system. When alcohol or narcotics enters the bloodstream the body boosts production of the neurotransmitter dopamine, which accounts for the pleasurable feeling of being high. Over time, the body requires more of the drug to reach the same state. The dependence that develops is separate from any psychological attachment. This is what I mean when I say that emotional trauma is at the heart of addiction but once the addiction is formed, the physical dependence acquires a life of its own. Therefore, the two components of addiction need to be treated in parallel. The truth is that every single addict grapples with emotional issues, and without treating both the addiction and the emotional issues simultaneously, addicts are doomed to relapse.

Some readers may be angered by my assertion that every addict suffers from underlying emotional issues. But my years of experience as a mental health professional who treats addicts has left me no doubt about this point, and I cannot underscore it strenuously enough: At the root of every addiction disorder is an emotional block.

Emotional trauma lies at the heart of every addiction.

Much of what we do at Creative Care centers on the tenets of what is called dual diagnosis, a label that today is used to describe people who suffer from both an addiction and a psychiatric disorder, including schizophrenia, clinical depression, bipolar disorder, and eating disorder. There are no limits to the possible combinations. Some are cocaine addicts who suffer from depression, some are alcoholics with panic disorder. Some are heroin addicts with borderline personality disorder. The severity of the emotional issues can vary, just as the degree of addiction can vary. For example, the emotional issue may be milder than the substance abuse issue. Meanwhile, a high-functioning alcoholic may suffer from a deeply entrenched anxiety issue.

There are common threads throughout the combinations. For starters, many addicts suffer from the same emotional issues, which are most commonly personality disorders, mood disorders, anxiety disorders, and psychotic disorders.

Also, many individuals find it impossible to recover from addiction for years because diagnosis of their coexisting emotional disorder is difficult. Although the concept that addicts suffer from dual disorders first emerged nearly 20 years ago, it is still not very well understood by the medical establishment. Exacerbating things is the fact that our healthcare system is not designed to treat dual disorders. The "system" has traditionally worked in two ways, neither of which is helpful to the dual diagnosis patient. In the first model, an individual is treated for one type of disorder at a time. In the second model, individuals are treated for both their emotional and addiction issues concurrently, but they see different doctors who struggle to "see the whole picture" of their patient, including how to treat him or her without exacerbating their other disorder.

Why are these the only options? Well, for example, in certain states like New York and California, medical insurance can only pay for patients' primary diagnosis—which often boils down to their most pressing problem when they meet with their doctor. (Never is it truer that timing is everything.)

Occasionally, the system's logic makes sense, particularly if an individual is suicidal. Obviously, then, substance abuse issues would take a backseat to the emotional issues at play. Generally speaking, though, it's virtually impossible for an individual with emotional issues and substance abuse issues to get all the help they need unless they can afford to pay out of their own pocket because medical providers can only charge insurers for one service.

Even the coverage for one piece or the other is often lousy. For example, insurance companies' coverage of substance-abuse treatment is typically extremely limited (usually up to 30 days in a treatment program or a maximum lifetime benefit). What is an individual struggling with addiction supposed to do once he or she has exceeded those arbitrary caps? It would be almost unimaginable if the healthcare industry treated other illnesses in the same way.

It's even harder to convince insurance companies to cover psychiatric treatment, as most coverage plans are designed instead with physical healthcare in mind.

Then there are those who are uninsured entirely, thanks in large part to eroding employer-based insurance. According to the most recent data from the U.S. Census Bureau, the number of uninsured Americans stood at an all-time high of 46.6 million in 2005. That's 5.4 million more people than lacked health insurance during the recession of 2001. Imagine the number of working poor who are battling dual disorders and who doctors and treatment centers will never see.

To those who don't understand the scope of the issue, sufferers seem unable to get well. As a result, they often lose their support systems, such as family and friends and whatever community keeps them grounded. This loss is not inconsequential: Without

support systems, all manner of bad things happen. Domestic violence increases, suicide attempts grow more common, and worse.
The remarkable thing is that once you know what signs to look
for, you realize that the spectrum of addiction is quite broad and
is everywhere. Nearly everyone knows someone who is an addict.
If you know that person well, you know he or she is also living in
a state of extreme emotional or psychological pain.

Consider this: According to the American Medical Association,
37 percent of alcohol abusers and 53 percent of drug abusers also
have at least one serious emotional illness. And of all people diagnosed as "mentally ill," 29 percent abuse either alcohol or drugs.
That's to say nothing of the many people like you and me who may
not have a classifiable condition but suffer from emotional issues
because of a trauma of some kind. Those emotional issues also
drive addiction, and unless they are addressed, an addict cannot
beat his or her addiction.

Thirty-seven percent of alcohol abusers and 53 percent of drug
abusers also have at least one serious emotional illness.

MISCONCEPTIONS ABOUT ADDICTION

There are a number of misconceptions regarding addiction. Let's
start with some background about addiction. Data from many
sources indicate that about 15 percent of the U.S. population
cannot drink responsibly, and approximately 5 to 10 percent of
male drinkers and 3 to 5 percent of female drinkers could be diagnosed as alcohol dependent. This adds up to roughly 12.5 million
people.[1] Adding nonalcoholic drugs into the mix bumps up that
estimate to roughly 22.2 million Americans who are currently

alcoholics or suffering from drug addiction.[2] Unfortunately, only 10 percent of the addicted population enters treatment.[3] And of the ones who seek help, only a small fraction, approximately 20 percent, achieves lasting recovery.

Most addicts relapse repeatedly, enduring long and frustrating journeys through various treatment options. They're left feeling helpless, confused, and broke—these treatments are costly.

Fifteen percent of the U.S. population cannot drink responsibly, and approximately 5 to 10 percent of male drinkers and 3 to 5 percent of female drinkers could be diagnosed as alcohol dependent.

Why does treatment have such a high failure rate? At Creative Care, we believe the problem is a widespread misunderstanding of the nature of addiction.

In the literature of Alcoholics Anonymous (AA), alcoholism is described as an "illness." AA didn't initiate the disease concept of alcoholism—rather the American Medical Association called it thus in 1950—but it is how most members describe their addiction. This has become the common view of addiction, despite a glut of critical research that argues against addiction being a disease.[4]

I would never condemn AA. On the contrary, AA was revolutionary in its time; it recognized addiction in a new light, and it let people come together and establish for themselves a place to be. It still provides a structure for people who need one another and can support each another for the rest of their lives.

Yet because addiction has come to be viewed as a physical condition akin to heart disease or diabetes, most people see little reason to delve into its psychological underpinnings.

Those specialists who do support the dual diagnosis model—psychiatrists or psychologists—rightly conclude that they can prepare the way for people to accept treatment by breaking down their resistance to the reality of their addiction.

It's a wonderful first step—getting people to acknowledge that they have a serious and potentially fatal problem. But the trouble with the "disease" model is that it doesn't address the emotional issues behind the addiction. In treatment programs, drug and alcohol counselors focus on pursuing AA's renowned 12 Steps program, a terrifically powerful group of related principles wherein addicts admit their subjection to alcohol, take a fearless inventory of themselves, and seek "through prayer and mediation to improve" their "conscious contact with God," as each individual understands him or her.

But most alcohol and drug recovery centers examine their clients' emotional history only as deeply as the 12 Step program requires—which is to say, not deeply.

The 12 Step program says: You are unhappy because you drink. Stop drinking, and your sobriety will give you happiness.

And certainly, people should be thankful and happy for every day that they are sober. But the reality is if you take away the drink, you still have problems. Sobriety doesn't instantly equal happiness. Addicts relapse because their cover gets taken away, and they're left miserable. It's largely why AA, which is highly effective for some people, has a one-year success rate of 31 percent and a longer-term success rate of roughly 35 percent when used as the sole treatment, according to AA, which surveys its members every few years.

As 57-year-old Andrew*—a father, businessman, and former patient of Creative Care whom you will meet in the next

---

* I have used pseudonyms for my former patients who have provided anecdotes for this book to protect their identities.

chapter—explains it: "In my life, I've had several wonderful drug and alcohol counselors, who've had my best interests in mind. But I went into rehab at two prominent clinics—and relapsed after both—before coming to Creative Care because I needed more than [those clinics] had to offer. Both did a great job of getting me clean, but there was no therapy whatsoever, and I had unresolved issues that were causing me to backslide time and again."

Others in the treatment community have an even more simplistic view of addiction than proponents of the disease model. In their view, it is the sufferer's own fault, and addicts are viewed collectively as weak-willed.

It is a sad reality that the first thing many addicts and alcoholics sacrifice in order to get and use their particular drug is their own sense of personal integrity. People who would never lie or steal turn into liars and thieves in order to feed their demon. But at certain religion-based treatment centers, alcoholism is presented as a moral failing, and at a greater number of broader-based centers, treatment has a moralistic tinge. For example, Therapeutic Communities—residential programs for heroin, cocaine, and marijuana addicts—often treat patients harshly. Rigid discipline and harsh punishment are believed to reshape addicts into good citizens. This draconian approach may work for a few people, but for most it does more harm than good.

Not last, there is the common view of addiction centers as expensive retreats for hedonists, Hollywood starlets, and shamed politicians in need of somewhere to disappear for a while. Many "rehab" facilities welcome such clients and do very little to help them. It's unfortunate for all treatment facilities, which get painted with the same broad brush by the media. But it's much worse for clients of those centers, who aren't getting what they desperately need: real help.

THE TRUTH ABOUT ADDICTION

In this book, you will learn that addiction is not a moral failing, that calling it a "disease" is misleading, and that far too often, the 12 Steps alone do not bring about lasting transformation. In order to recover, you or someone you care about needs much more.

Consider that while research strongly suggests that alcoholism has at least a small physical component, and while numerous family and twin studies have shown that some individuals appear to have a genetic propensity toward alcoholism, no study has yet proved this conclusively. There is some evidence that alcoholism is inherited, but science has yet to find the direct genetic link.

More to the point, inheriting the propensity to become an addict doesn't necessarily make a person an addict. We all know people who can drink socially or prefer not to drink at all even though their parents or grandparents had chemical dependencies. Emotional and sometimes psychiatric issues—occasionally but not always in conjunction with a genetic tendency—are the true driving forces of addiction.

The emotional issue in question might be depression and anxiety. Often these issues spring in part from some kind of trauma that need not be as dramatic as violent physical or sexual abuse. Simply watching your parents fighting, night after night, might constitute trauma.

Whether an event constitutes a trauma depends on the individual, since some people are more sensitive to the effects of painful events than others. The same negative experience could leave one person psychologically unscathed but might devastate another person, driving him or her to drugs and alcohol. Many of our success stories at Creative Care have involved helping patients who have been able to make connections between what is happening today and significant trauma in their lives.

The emotional issue may also stem from a chemical imbalance as seemingly innocuous as too much or too little adrenaline. Too much adrenaline causes feelings of nervousness and anxiety and an inability to relax. Some people can live that way; others find themselves self-medicating with alcohol or other depressants. Too little adrenaline can create its own issues, such as feelings of fatigue, which causes some who are unhappy with their lethargy to seek out and use stimulants like the crystalline alkaloid cocaine and the stimulant methamphetamine (better known as crystal meth).

The list of emotional issues that fuel addiction issues is long indeed. For example, at Creative Care, we also treat addicts with eating disorders, both anorexia and bulimia. There are many similarities between the compulsive abuse of food and the compulsive abuse of alcohol or drugs. Both involve the loss of control, shame, secrecy, as well as disregard for the obvious health problems that result. And both can lead to substance abuse. Bulimics, who typically have impulse control issues, often binge on food after bingeing on alcohol, and then vomit up what they can. Meanwhile, anorexics tend to use stimulants to keep off weight and to control their appetite. Although anorexics most commonly use the stimulants caffeine and nicotine, they sometimes use cocaine or other illegal substances.

Sometimes the emotional issue driving the alcohol or drug abuse is far less obvious than the impulse control problem. A study conducted at the University of Indiana[5] argued that "behavioral disinhibition," or boldness of character, essentially, can heighten the probability that someone—particularly with a family history of substance abuse—will become a substance abuser.

An uninhibited person may be characterized by "an apparent insensitivity to punishment, an increased sensitivity to immediate rewards . . . and a failure to consider and inhibit behavior when aversive consequences are likely."

Some people are born with behavioral disinhibition. Children and adolescents who were exposed to alcohol in the womb sometimes have altered brain regions. According to a recent study by San Diego State University researchers, those altered brain regions sometimes result in changes to their behavior, including causing inattention and behavioral disinhibition.[6] Indeed, according to the study, individuals with fetal alcohol syndrome are at greater risk for attention deficit hyperactivity disorder and other psychiatric diseases linked with poor inhibitory control.

The scientists conducting the study examined 175 male and female nonalcoholics between the ages of 18 and 30, roughly half of whom had a family history involving alcoholism. They wrote: "Those high in behavioral disinhibition are probably more likely to experiment with substance use earlier, because they are less inhibited by the prospect of negative consequences and less likely to learn to moderate their consumption once they have initiated use."

Either way, once an addiction has developed, it becomes an ingrained habit—a separate condition with a life of its own. So the addict has not one but two problems: the addiction itself and the underlying issues that largely caused it in the first place.

Ten years ago, most treatment clinics treated emotional problems as symptoms arising from the substance abuse. They would conclude that, for example, a man who was angry and an alcoholic was angry *because* of his abuse of alcohol, which brought out his worst qualities. And though this person might be convinced to stop drinking—having been told that his depressive qualities would disappear when he was sober—he would most likely relapse.

Today we know that angry alcoholics might have a neuro-chemical imbalance that they have been medicating with alcohol. We know how the two issues, a chemical imbalance and alcoholism, become linked, and they are very tricky—but not impossible—to untangle and treat.

EMOTIONS AND ADDICTION

Again, to answer the question of how often it is that chemically dependent people have underlying emotional issues, major or minor: it is always. Someone with underlying psychiatric issues is, unfortunately, at much greater risk of turning to alcohol and drugs than someone who doesn't have those issues. Examples of emotional issues that drive addiction include major depression combined with cocaine addiction, alcohol addiction combined with panic disorder, alcoholism and/or drug addiction with schizophrenia, and borderline personality disorder with episodic drug abuse. But there are many other scenarios, and all of them are rife with danger for the sufferer.

According to the National Institutes of Health, which is part of the U.S. Department of Health and Human Services, a person who experiences a major depressive episode is four times more likely to succumb to substance abuse. Similarly, someone with a panic disorder is at four times greater risk. A person with obsessive-compulsive disorder is three and a half times more likely to become an alcoholic or drug abuser. And someone suffering from schizophrenia is ten times more likely to drink or take drugs.

At even greater risk are individuals who suffer from manic episodes; their chances of becoming substance abusers are 14.5 times higher than average. Antisocial personality disorder increases someone's chances of becoming an addict by a whopping 15.5 percent.

You might be thinking of the age-old chicken-and-egg conundrum and wondering if substance abuse can create emotional problems. The answer is yes. Although many people "self-medicate"—as when people whose bodies produce too much adrenaline turn to alcohol or other depressants to feel calmer, or when those who feel down take stimulants to feel more lively—taking too many drugs or relying on alcohol for too long can, particularly in teenagers, cause emotional problems in adulthood, including severe depression.

CREATIVE CARE'S TREATMENT

Studies have also shown that drugs and alcohol can cause anxiety owing to their pharmacological values and that once their use is under control or stops, the anxiety dissipates.

Recovery always is a difficult process, beginning with detoxification, during which the body cleanses itself of drugs or alcohol. Detox usually takes a painful four to seven days. Examinations for other medical problems are necessary while detox is in full swing. Liver and blood clotting problems are the most common issues, though sometimes fatal complications can occur, such as delirium tremens, a severe form of alcohol withdrawal that involves sudden and severe mental or neurological changes.

The good news is that once a person has gone through detox, he or she can begin treatment for the alcohol or drug problem and for the emotional issue.

Recovery for a substance abuse problem usually involves individual and group psychotherapy, education about alcohol and drugs, and participation in the 12 Steps.

Treatment for an emotional issue depends on the diagnosis. I'll discuss these in much greater detail in later chapters, but for most disorders, individual and group therapy works best. Intensive individual therapy can work wonders in teaching addicts how to deal with cues that entice them to use (cues that can be overwhelming). Support groups of other people who are recovering from the same condition are also incredibly helpful. As we've all experienced, when in turmoil, there's nothing so reassuring as realizing that we aren't alone in our problems and that others with the same issues have found, or are finding, a way to overcome them.

Therapies that allow people to express themselves in new ways are also helpful. At Creative Care, our patients often partake in writing and art therapy, including journaling and reading assignments.

We also ask our patients to participate in mindfulness meditation and in equine-assisted therapy. In this therapy, patients establish relationships with horses; the horses' reactions can make people aware of their own emotional states.

Another less conventional therapeutic approach that we have found effective is simply solitude—being alone for up to two hours. We specifically promote this downtime because recovering addicts are very anxious; they want all of their time accounted for. And the majority of recovery programs offer them exactly that. Every half hour is scheduled with group therapy and educational sessions and other meetings, from daybreak to lights out.

We don't overschedule. We let patients sit with themselves, because as long as you're busy, you're avoiding. It's terribly important to sit and look inside yourself and learn to love yourself again. As Julia, a former Creative Care patient whom you will meet later in the book, explains, "When you're in recovery, spending time alone can be the hardest time of every day because you don't like yourself and no one wants to think about that. But the goal is for you to learn to be by yourself and enjoy yourself, because if you can't do it [in rehab], how are you going to do it in the outside world?"

Creative Care has also become a valuable resource for other substance abuse clinics, including the esteemed alcohol and drug addiction treatment organizations Hazelden and the Betty Ford Center. Both focus on providing alcohol and other drug dependency treatment services. Patients who require more intensive psychotherapeutic treatment than those organizations are designed to provide often come to Creative Care.

Indeed, it is with great pride that we take on some of the toughest cases of addiction: patients whose treatment has proved sufficiently challenging that other clinics see us as a crucial piece of their recovery process.

HOW FAMILIES CAN ASSIST IN RECOVERY

The addiction recovery process is exceedingly complicated. Often medication—the right medication, taken as indicated—is critical. Family can also be a key part of the recovery process, particularly once family members fully understand the problems and accept the underlying emotional issue. The greater their awareness, the better the chances their son or daughter or mother or father has of enjoying a lasting recovery.

As you will read throughout this book, the family component of recovery can be a complicated one. In some cases, family members have unwittingly enabled their loved ones to pursue their addictions, including by providing financial support and by making excuses on their behalf. Sometimes families simply turn a blind eye to their loved one's problems, clinging to the delusion that the behavior is fleeting or that it derives from a more socially acceptable cause: immaturity or stress or a bad mate. Sometimes families cut off their loved ones entirely to protect themselves from their distress and what can sometimes seem like all-consuming neediness. In such cases, during the recovery of the child or spouse or parent, the family member or members must learn to stop their own damaging behaviors when contact with the addict is resumed. Often well-meaning family members say things that addicts interpret as overly intrusive or overly critical, which can increase stress and cause them to self-medicate again.

The good news is that when relatives are taught about an addict's disorder or disorders, they gain a greater understanding of how to accept the situation and relate to their loved ones in healthier ways. Additionally, when families are taught how to communicate more effectively, often there is often far less stress involved in the relationship, and much more support, and the likelihood of relapse drops dramatically.

In fact, a strong emotional connectedness among family members is by far one of the most powerful tools in the process of recovery.

A recent patient at Creative Care illustrates my point. The patient—we'll call him Martin—is now on the path to wellness, thanks largely to his family, who helped us "raise the bottom" for him.

What do I mean by "raising the bottom?" As counterintuitive as it may seem, the worse patients get, the better their chances of a full recovery. Many people need to hit bottom before they are willing to wholly surrender to treatment. Unfortunately, in far too many cases, an individual's real "bottom" is death. At Creative Care, we do what we can to make patients aware that what they most value in life is going to be lost to them, if it isn't already.

Strong emotional ties with family members is one of the most powerful tools in the recovery process.

In Martin's case, we made it very clear that Gwenyth, his wife of 15 years, was preparing to walk out on him and had already met with an attorney regarding how to divide their assets. Worried that Martin would immediately stop his treatment, she had sought to hide this information from her husband while he was in recovery.

We made it clear that not only would he lose his beloved partner but that the career that was of such importance to him (and which he was slowly destroying) would blow up entirely. Finally, we helped him to realize what he was doing to his relationship with the couple's teenage daughter. She barely knew her father and claimed, in family therapy sessions at Creative Care, to have lost interest in getting to know him. That sentiment couldn't have been further from the truth, of course.

The work wasn't easy. Martin didn't have an epiphany. His outlook didn't change overnight. But over time, through the education that our trained staff provided him and the support of his daughter and wife, Martin came to comprehend that he was on the brink of losing the people he loved most in the world and the career that he had once worked so hard to shape. We also helped him to understand that he could still do something to avoid that outcome. Every day, he continues to work at doing exactly that.

CHILDREN AND THE RECOVERY PROCESS

A quick side note about young children and the recovery process: In the course of treatment, we take a look at the entire family. If a mother has, say, been using in front of her children, or if her children have seen her doing things that no child should see a parent doing, we'll make appropriate referrals to a child therapist or psychologist. We can't force children to seek treatment, but we can and do make recommendations if we believe that it is needed.

If the addict has managed to keep secret his or her problems— and this is usually only the case with very young children—we typically advise leaving children out of the recovery process. In fact, it's highly counterproductive and damaging when, during the process, a spouse or guardian tries using the addict's children as brakes, hoping to motivate the addict to slow or quit drug or alcohol use. Using children in this way seldom works. Even when a child perceives that something is wrong, the insecurity inherent in having a parent with an active addition only exacerbates that child's sense of destabilization in most cases.

As with Martin's daughter, older children may find it hard to love and care about a parent who is self-destructive. Individual therapy followed by groups that help family and friends of addicts, such as Al-Anon, can be very useful in helping family members cope and learn how to set healthy boundaries for themselves.

Once the addict is firmly committed to and engaged in the recovery process, visits with children can be a healthy experience for everyone concerned.

THE IMPORTANCE OF TERMINOLOGY

You may have noticed that I have not referred—nor will I ever refer—to people's emotional disorders as "mental illness." Fear of stigma too often prevents addicts from seeking treatment. While it is hard for patients to admit to a substance abuse problem, it's even harder for them to admit to struggling with what is popularly referred to as "mental illness"—that is, emotional and psychiatric issues. And no wonder, since a common misconception is that so-called mental illness is the sufferers' own fault.

The sad fact is that many people still do not see emotional and psychiatric issues as legitimate medical problems. Instead, they see such issues as something that individuals could "get over" if they really tried. Because we cannot point to a single physical cause for such issues, some people assume that the problems are all in the sufferer's head. Like addiction, too often people see emotional and psychiatric issues as fundamental failures of will.

The term "mental illness" helps sustain this stigma. The word "illness" summons unpleasant thoughts of contagion. Equally bad, the phrase creates a false division between the "mentally healthy" or "normal" people and the "mentally ill"—or between "us" and "them."

Fear of being stigmatized all too often prevents addicts from seeking treatment.

I want to broaden the definition of mental disorder or condition. In fact, mental "health" is a spectrum of various states. There are people who have severe psychiatric issues at one end and people considered "normal" at the other who do not exhibit destructive behavior but who might still be struggling with emotional issues of some sort.

To some, this idea of a continuum is disconcerting. If those struggling with emotional and psychiatric issues are on the same spectrum as "normal" people, then there's less to stop us from becoming one of them. It's much less frightening to label sufferers as "mentally imbalanced" and imagine them as radically different from ourselves.

Obviously, the two ends of this spectrum are far apart. There is a big difference between those struggling with schizophrenia or severe trauma and the average person who may occasionally battle anxiety or depression. This difference is in part due to the fact that major psychiatric conditions are often caused by biochemical imbalances.

Many of those whom we designate as "mentally ill" are struggling with problems that are different from those of "ordinary people," chiefly in their magnitude. There is no clear-cut distinction between "us" and "them." We are them. As for those who have severe psychiatric disorders—those at the extreme end of the spectrum—the term "mental illness" obscures their humanity and oversimplifies a complex condition.

A new terminology is needed if our thinking is to change. Although "emotional issues" may seem euphemistic, it's a euphemism with a purpose. The less stigma there is, the more likely we all are to admit to our problems and get treatment for them. And without outdated terminology to constrain us, the more likely it is that our thinking about these problems will evolve.

3

How Emotional Pain Can Lead to Addiction

THE CLINICAL PROFESSION HAS agreed for many years that people drink or abuse drugs in an attempt to numb the pain from the emotional problems afflicting them. Yet the popular imagination mistakenly believes that once the core of the trauma is identified, the chemical addiction will evaporate instantly. I do believe that emotional trauma is the seed from which an addiction grows, but I disagree that the road to health is a simple matter of solving a mystery. Addiction is a symptom of an underlying problem, but it's a symptom that alters the biochemistry of the body. Once substance abuse develops, it becomes an independent problem. You might compare it to bacteria infecting a wound. By the time the tissue is colonized by invading organisms, it's not enough simply to bandage the wound. You must treat the infection separately.

Similarly, once an addiction has developed, it takes on a life of its own. This is because addicts respond automatically to cues, or reminders of their drug or alcohol use, long after they have tackled their emotional issues. Research has shown that when cocaine addicts see someone using coke, their levels of dopamine—the neurotransmitter, a chemical that transmits nerve impulses, that cocaine elevates—actually increase in anticipation. So no matter how much a person has labored to heal underlying wounds, a stimulus still may activate the urge to use again.

Emotional trauma is the seed from which addiction grows.

Because the path to breaking a drug or alcohol habit is so challenging, I'm going to let some of my former patients—some of the many people I've successfully treated in 25 years of clinical experience—tell you their stories directly. Through their own words, you will see that their simultaneous battles against addiction and emotional demons were not easy.

One part of the challenge is that in many cases, patients become attached to their traumas—they come to identify themselves by them. That is true of several people whom you will meet in these pages.

But as you read their stories, I hope that you will be inspired as they find the answers they need to survive.

ANDREW'S STORY

The first case in point is Andrew, who came to us in a crisis in midlife. At first glance, Andrew appeared to have it all. The child of a billionaire real estate developer in the Midwest, Andrew, the middle of seven children, characterizes his upbringing as

"Rockefelleresque. We had the big house, a dog, a backyard, and every creature comfort."

They had much more than that, yet Andrew—today a bespectacled 57-year-old with blond-gray hair and a measured, professorial way of speaking—wound up in and out of treatment facilities for years. Why? Andrew had a paternal uncle who had died of alcoholism and his maternal grandmother "liked pills," as he once put it, but otherwise, he had no reason to live in fear of addiction.

So what drove him to drink? Here are the emotional origins of his addictions, in in his own words.

> My family is right-wing Evangelical. My father was a successful businessman. My mother was a stay-at-home mom; she really raised us because my father was gone a lot on business trips or else would typically arrive home after dinner.
>
> Mom was terrific. I spent a lot of time with her. She was always very supportive, very loving. She spent time disproportionately with some of the kids, in truth, and I think I was her favorite.

He meanwhile characterizes his father as "very much an authoritarian figure."

> Dad would attend certain school functions as time allowed—parent–teacher meetings, Boy Scouts—but his parenting technique was really crisis intervention in that he'd fix the squeaky wheel—attend to whichever child most needed him.
>
> I preferred it that way. I was almost fearful of him. Checking in felt like a progress report, and I never wanted to disappoint him, so if I didn't have anything happening that might impress him, I just wanted to avoid that interaction.

Andrew calls his childhood "typically uneventful."

> *I was an Eagle Scout. I served on student council. I was a
> good kid, although I smoked pot for the first time my sopho-
> more year of high school, with my older brother's girlfriend,
> and I knew immediately that I liked it; it absolutely diminished
> my anxiety. I was very shy. But it didn't become a regular
> thing. I never sought it out or bought any.*

Life, as Andrew would tell you, was wholly unremarkable until the
summer of his junior year. He'd been a strong student at a competitive public school in an affluent suburb of Chicago, but after
attending a summer program at a boarding school in Connecticut,
where he did exceptionally well, his parents were encouraged to
send him to the school for his senior year.

Andrew wasn't sold on the school itself, but as he was shy and
unpopular at his public high school, he decided to take advantage
of the opportunity and switch to a different school.

> *The particular prep school where I'd spent the summer hadn't
> done much for me, but I was interested in a small private school
> in New Hampshire because it had a boxing program and a ski
> program and I had a sister, with a car, at the University of New
> Hampshire, which was very appealing to me.*

Andrew's parents were happy to send him where he wanted to go,
but once at the boarding school, his focus was less on academics
and more on drugs, a preoccupation for many of his new classmates.

> *The real education I got at boarding school was a drug
> education. The other kids there had already established rela-
> tionships, cliques. I was an outsider stepping in and so wound*

up becoming friends with several guys who were heavy drug users. My schedule evolved into classes, then study hall, then drug use in the evening. I tried a little bit of everything except cocaine: LSD, mescaline, psychedelic mushrooms, pot. I liked it all except the LSD. Nothing like making yourself more paranoid in an already highly controlled environment.

When Andrew graduated, he went on to a private college in Southern California. It was attended by the children of other accomplished businessmen and taught by teachers who lived on campus and acted as surrogate parents. Andrew pledged the only fraternity on campus.

The college was just a vehicle for partying. I don't think I was sober for half of hazing week. I was happy at how easy it was to make friends there.

Not surprisingly, my grades were terrible; I wasn't focused. By my third year, it was obvious to both me and my family that my focus wasn't on academics, and we agreed that I should stop wasting time and figure out what I was going to be when I grew up. So I eagerly took a year off and worked for one of our many family businesses, a hotel chain based in Florida.

I guess that's when the real trouble started. The job was international in scope, and for the first six months, I traveled to London and Paris for installations of our hotels' particular key system, which was initially flawed. That meant lots of getting up in the middle of the night to help the hotels' front desks. To cope, I started using cocaine to stay up and Quaaludes to go back to sleep.

When I finally moved back to Florida on a more full-time basis, I started using even more. I was lonely. I didn't know

*anyone outside the company, and as part of the
executive office, I wasn't very approachable within the
company.*

Andrew says that he "didn't like the drugs, but I found them effective. I looked at them purely as tools." Except that he was taking
so many that by now he had a serious problem. He met with a
local therapist, who encouraged him to go to a treatment facility.

> *On her suggestion, I went to a clinic in Leesburg, Virginia,
> where I spent five weeks. I stopped using while I was there, but
> it wasn't a meaningful experience. I wasn't looking for spiritu-
> ality; I just wanted to break the cycle. Also, the AA meetings
> were populated by hard-core alcoholics who weren't interested
> in my drug use. They were very intolerant of anything having
> to do with drugs. As far as they were concerned, I wasn't an
> alcoholic and had no place at their meetings. That was okay,
> though it turned me off to AA.*

Andrew left treatment feeling unready emotionally to work again
full time. So he returned to his small college, and graduated.

Afterward, Andrew had many options from which to choose,
thanks to his family connections. He decided on a family business
based in New York.

> *This time I was in charge of a real estate venture with some of
> our New York partners. The idea was to set up a massive
> property in New Jersey where various healthcare providers
> would open up storefronts alongside a continuing education
> center and a hotel.*
>
> *Unfortunately, one of our attorneys, whose office was next
> to mine in New York, was a cocaine addict, and it didn't take*

him long to convince me to snort it with him on the job, so coke was suddenly reintroduced into my life.

It was hard to resist. Like life in Florida, I was lonely in New York. I was just getting to know my wife—at the time my girlfriend—but she was busy with her career. The only other friends I had then were the children of some family friends, and they were heavy cocaine users, too.

I somehow managed to keep my coke use under the radar during this period, partly because I was developing a bifurcated life. In addition to our project in New Jersey, I'd gotten involved in yet another business venture in Connecticut. Because I was out of New York so often, I could easily misbehave.

That cycle ended only after I came home from a trip out to Connecticut to find one of my sisters and her daughter at our home in New York City. I picked up my niece, but I'd done a bit of coke and was off balance and in danger of dropping her for a split second, and that was it. My wife saw the whole thing and she immediately launched an investigation. The first thing she found was a small stash in my briefcase. She just walked right over to me, stared me down, and said, "This is done."

Within 24 hours I was in rehab at [another clinic in Malibu], where I spent the next 28 days and where I finally came to terms with the reality that I was an addict.

We had an intensive family therapy visit there, with my six siblings and wife, and we did "listing," where you tell someone, "When you do this, I feel such and such." Every member of your family gets a turn. Well, in my family, we're all Type A, all alpha, all leaders, and it came out how competitive our family is, mostly to please our father.

It was an amazing experience. Until then, we'd all been operating under the false premise that everything was great, *but really, my brother wanted to list my father, my sister wanted to list my mother, and so on.*

Though Andrew speaks with a laugh about the experience now, his stay at the treatment clinic was so powerful that he remained sober for the next eight years. His marriage flourished. He and his wife had two children. He was engaged in work.

Andrew was sure that he'd never touch alcohol or drugs again, in fact. Then the unexpected happened.

I'd left treatment with fear around addiction, and I was stone sober for the next eight years. But then I was hit by a car as I was crossing the street in London, where I was on a business trip. I flew through the windshield. I broke a few bones but the worst of it was the horrific back pain I felt for the next two years. In fact, within nine months of the accident—which required three surgeries, including spinal fusion to combine and immobilize several vertebrae—I was addicted to just about every pain medication out there: OxyContin, Percocet, Vicodin. It was all medically indicated, but I had so many different doctors working on me at the time that getting more than I needed was no problem at all.

At the same time that Andrew was struggling with pain management and a growing awareness that he was once again in the throes of an addiction he couldn't control, one of the projects in which he had been involved was falling apart.

Seizing the opportunity created by Andrew's prolonged absence, his chief financial officer and a contractor embezzled $8 million. When Andrew finally realized what had happened, he called his family's attorneys. He also committed to getting himself to a treatment facility. With his wife's support, he checked himself into a renowned addiction clinic. But its program focuses solely on addiction and not the underlying emotional issues that drive it, so, as Andrew would later say:

> It does a great job of getting you clean, but there's no therapy whatsoever, so though I went through 28 days and cleaned up, I still wasn't engaged in a program of recovery. This time, it took just a year for me to relapse. I was still dealing with the fallout from the embezzlement, with forensic accountants, trying to nail those guys. I felt just horrible. I'd trusted these people, I'd hired them, and I felt violated and used and, frankly, stupid.

A year later, Andrew was again hooked and abusing OxyContin, Xanax, and Ambien.

Conservative radio host Rush Limbaugh's problem with OxyContin has brought the painkiller to public awareness. OxyContin is a narcotic analgesic used for pain relief associated with injuries, bursitis, and arthritis, but people can easily manipulate the controlled release formulation for a powerful, morphine-like high. Xanax, a popular benzodiazepine—or "benzo"—is typically used to treat severe anxiety disorders and sometimes clinical depression. Benzos typically are prescribed only for short periods because they are potentially addictive, and the longer people take them, the more benzos they need to take to experience the same result. Meanwhile, Ambien is commonly prescribed to treat insomnia. (The United States Air Force uses it to help pilots sleep after a flight mission.) Medicinal use can turn into abuse, however, when people take it longer than the prescribed four-to-six weeks or, as in Andrew's case, when people who've been dependent on drugs or alcohol in the past begin using it.

Fortunately, Andrew now realized that he needed more than just addiction therapy: He had unresolved issues that were causing him to backslide. He was also coming to terms with those issues, thanks to the help of a therapist he'd begun seeing. For example, she helped show Andrew that he had deep insecurities and suffered from a severe lack of self-esteem. In addition, he was intimidated by the environment in which he'd grown up and was overwhelmed by expectations, both real and imagined.

What Andrew still needed to do was connect those issues to his addictions. A pragmatist, he felt it would be overindulgent to blame his childhood for his repeated failures to stay sober. It was then that Andrew's cousin, who had once been a patient at Creative Care, pointed him in our direction. At our facility, he finally found a way to connect the dots between his trauma and his addictions.

What happened is that at Creative Care, I finally resigned my role of prodigal son.

It started with more intensive group therapy than I'd ever had, with morning groups, afternoon groups, meetings in the evenings. I also visited with my primary care therapist three times a week. I wrote letters to my father. I know I wrote and rewrote the same letter six times at one point. I never sent them, but they were therapeutic and they helped me realize, when the time was right, that I really needed to invite my father to the clinic, which I did.

And you know what? I told him everything that I'd never been able to say to him before, for fear that he'd think me whiny or unappreciative or ridiculous. For fear that I'd be wasting his time.

I told him that I wanted no part of any of our family's businesses anymore. I told him that I was tired of reporting to him as the president of a company, tired of talking about profit and loss statements. It was a huge, pivotal point for me, resigning my role. I said, "I want to be a person you take in an interest in outside of business, and I want you to let me in; I want to know you better, too." That meeting was two years ago, and it made all the difference in the world.

Andrew's case really underscores the power of daily therapy, which all of our patients receive, both in group sessions and with a primary therapist who is assigned to them. For his entire life, Andrew had been tormented by the belief that his father didn't hold him in high regard. He was certain that his father didn't think he was intelligent, and that his father didn't respect him because he didn't have the wherewithal to stay in recovery. By finally coming to understand those fears and express them, we, along with Andrew's father, were able to disabuse him of such deeply rooted, and destructive, fears.

Equally as important, Andrew listened to us. He was very resentful of how much therapy we were asking him to undergo at the outset. But within weeks, he was very grateful to us. It's not a credit to us but to him that he knew that to regain control of his life, he had to hand over the reins for a while, to examine his old ways of thinking about his relationship with his father, and even to stay with us longer than he'd expected when we recognized that he had more work left to do.

Today, my father and I have the relationship that I always craved, and it makes me unspeakably happy. I'm so glad I took a stand when I did because otherwise, I might have missed my opportunity. Having his open support has made an enormous difference in how I feel about my life. Also, though I always considered myself a good parent to my kids, my connection to my father has really opened up parts of me that I didn't realize were closed off.

Andrew now calls the last two years the "best of my life. I think of myself now as a terrific parent, husband, and boss." Since his stay at Creative Care, he has shed his family-related business obligations and begun a new career as an entertainment producer, a role he loves. He is also taking much better care of himself: biking, running, and generally being more productive than ever.

Not last, he now says that when "anything presents as a crossroad, I call up my AA sponsor. I call up other friends. I have more reasons not to succumb." Andrew also knows "never to fool myself into thinking anything other than that the disease is front and center and that you never know what will wake it up."

THE VOID THAT WILL NOT HEAL

Emotional trauma does not have to result from the impact of a particular incident. As you saw from Andrew's story, he was not subject to a particularly painful event, such as physical or sexual abuse. But his relationship with his father undermined Andrew psychologically, and Andrew turned to narcotics to fill the void of that ambivalent parental love.

Each of us can probably identify a void in our lives that comes back to bite us when we experience upheavals in other parts of our lives.

Addictive behavior is just one way we punish ourselves for our vulnerabilities.

4

❧

Recognizing Addictive Behavior

*H*OW DO YOU KNOW if someone you care about is addicted? There are a great many misconceptions about addiction, and they often form the basis for excuses to not enter treatment. One of the most common misconceptions is: "I'm not an addict because I have a home and a family." But drug addiction and alcoholism are hardly phenomena relegated to skid row. If anything, there are probably many more addicts who are virtually indistinguishable from everyone else—save that they drink or continue their drug use no matter how adverse the consequences.

"But I go to work every day" is another popular excuse. Behind it lies the common belief that you can be a "functioning alcoholic" or "social drug user"—the idea that as long as you're still employed and bringing home a paycheck, you can carry on with your "vice." In fact, even if your drinking or drug use isn't impacting your work attendance, it is doubtless causing a host of other problems—or it will soon. Many recovering individuals will tell you that it's a short path from managing to get by to finding it difficult to get to the office at all.

"I'm not an alcoholic/drug abuser because I don't use around the clock. Sometimes I don't use every day." That's another common excuse. The reality is that some alcoholics really *don't* drink very often. They can go days, weeks, or even months without having a drop of alcohol—feats they brag about, as if abstaining for short periods underscores that they aren't addicts. The problem, as those close to them (and, ultimately, as they themselves) know is that they have zero control over their alcohol consumption or drug use once they return to it.

Another common excuse for not seeking treatment is: "It's my business if I drink; it's only my own life that I'm screwing up." It's essential for addicts to understand that their behavior affects the lives of their loved ones as well as their own. Talking with family and friends can help here. Eventually, every addict must acknowledge that addiction is at the root of his or her problems, not bad luck or abuse by others (although these may play a role, of course).

Taking responsibility is liberating, because if people can accept that they have the power to create a bad situation, they can grasp that it's within their power to change the situation.

Specific to alcoholism, there's also the old excuse of: "I know I drink a lot, but it doesn't affect me," or "I have to drink a lot because my tolerance for alcohol is high. It doesn't mean I'm an alcoholic." Again, the argument simply doesn't reflect reality.

Alcoholism typically develops over a period of time in which an individual consumes more and more alcohol. It's true that people who have been increasing their alcohol consumption over time become more tolerant before they notice the effects of alcohol. There is a tipping point, however. Tolerance leads to memory lapses and then, typically, a lack of control so that people can no longer stop when they want or even when they need to do so. Often these people have no idea that they've become alcoholics until they're faced by a situation that demands their full, sober attention, such as a spouse who is threatening to leave, or a friend in need, or job loss. Of course, by then, usually a considerable amount of damage has been done already.

"It's healthy to drink every day; it's why the French live as long as they do." Believe it or not, we've heard this excuse, too. And you know what? Taken literally, it's true. Many researchers believe that moderate alcohol consumption actually can protect against cardiovascular diseases. Of course, those researchers are talking about no more than two glasses of wine or beer a day for women and up to three glasses of one or the other for men. It's when two or three drinks become four and six that the risk of a number of diseases, including cirrhosis of the liver, goes through the roof. And that's to say nothing about the other physical problems caused by excessive alcohol consumption, including sleeping disorders, hypertension, breast and other cancers, and dementia.

Sometimes it is easier to put addiction into perspective by answering those questions that people might sooner avoid.

We've found that one of the most useful surveys for alcoholics/ addicts is one compiled by the National Council on Alcoholism and Drug Dependence[1]—a very helpful organization first established in 1944 to battle "the stigma and the disease of alcoholism and other drug addictions." The survey was created to help individuals recognize whether they have a drinking problem. Take a look at the questions and give them some thought.

1. Do you occasionally drink heavily after a disappointment, a quarrel, or when the boss gives you a hard time?

2. When you have trouble or feel under pressure, do you always drink more heavily than usual?

3. Have you noticed that you are able to handle more liquor than you did when you were first drinking?

4. Did you ever wake up on the morning after and discover that you could not remember part of the evening before, even though your friends tell you that you did not pass out?

5. When drinking with other people, do you try to have a few extra drinks when others will not know it?

6. Are there certain occasions when you feel uncomfortable if alcohol is not available?

7. Have you recently noticed that when you begin drinking you are in a more of a hurry to get the first drink than you used to be?

8. Do you sometimes feel a little guilty about your drinking?

9. Are you secretly irritated when your family or friends discuss your drinking?

10. Have you recently noticed an increase in the frequency of your memory "blackouts"?

11. Do you often find that you wish to continue drinking after your friends say they have had enough?

12. Do you usually have a reason for the occasions when you drink heavily?

13. When you are sober, do you often regret things you have done or said while drinking?

14. Have you tried switching brands or following different plans for controlling your drinking?

15. Have you often failed to keep the promises you have made to yourself about controlling or cutting down on your drinking?

16. Have you ever tried to control your drinking by making a change in jobs, or moving to a new location?

17. Do you try to avoid family or close friends while you are drinking?

18. Are you having an increasing number of financial and work problems?

19. Do more people seem to be treating you unfairly without good reason?

20. Do you eat very little or irregularly when you are drinking?

21. Do you sometimes have the shakes in the morning and find that it helps to have a little drink?

22. Have you recently noticed that you cannot drink as much as you once did?

23. Do you sometimes stay drunk for several days at a time?

24. Do you sometimes feel very depressed and wonder whether life is worth living?

25. Sometimes after periods of drinking, do you see or hear things that aren't there?

26. Do you get terribly frightened after you have been drinking heavily?

IDENTIFYING CAUSE AND EFFECT

Overcoming denial also involves identifying the causal link between addiction and its negative consequences.

Addicts often start drinking or taking drugs for the reasons that people commonly do: to feel more sociable and at ease, and because everybody else does it. At some point, however, likely they begin to drink to forget their problems. It might even work a few times. Or, at least, the alcohol certainly feels like it's ameliorating those problems, as it stimulates certain areas of the brain that are responsible for thinking and pleasure seeking.

In fact, drugs and alcohol not only exacerbate existing problems, they create entirely new ones: emotional, familial, and physical, including conditions I just outlined, such as hypertension.

The emotional cause-and-effect patterns of addiction are fairly boilerplate. Almost always, addicts begin to avoid others, leading to feelings of isolation. Ashamed, addicts then begin abusing even more aggressively, further alienating themselves.

Much of the psychological impact from addiction stems from the person's sense of being a slave, whether to drugs or alcohol. Sometimes addicts come to recognize how unable they are to gain control of themselves only when they realize that their behavior completely contradicts long-held personal beliefs and values. It's not fun for addicts to know on some level the kind of mess they are creating and the serious and often unfixable toll it is taking on every aspect of their lives.

Indeed, after a point, the reality of their actions becomes inescapable—despite the fact that addicts often report trying harder and harder to "escape"—and that failure has its own related emotional consequences. It begins with feelings of depression and helplessness, then evolves into anxiety, which can manifest itself as general fearfulness or downright paranoia.

Addicts' feelings of low self-esteem and self-loathing increase over time as they retreat further and further from everyone else. Add a dose of depression and anger—which can cause someone to be touchy, then irritated, then sometimes a downright menace—with a splash of extreme boredom (because the pattern of addiction becomes so tediously predictable), and you have the makings of terribly unhappy people.

Psychologically, addiction has other impacts, too, including on the way that addicts process information. Specifically, addicts' thought patterns typically kick into defensive overdrive in order to protect their addiction. Addicts might first believe that someone can enter the picture and fix them. Without that happening, they convince themselves—and often others—that the addiction "isn't what it seems." Meanwhile, their focus on getting their drug of choice usually narrows to the point that nothing—and no one—matters as much as getting enough of it.

Finally, at some point, addicts who start to feel the consequences of their actions start contemplating doing whatever is necessary to stop themselves and end their pain, which often includes thoughts of self-harm.

Once addicts see the connection between substance abuse and other problems, it becomes much harder for them to put off treatment. Once realism enters the picture, the equivocations and excuses—"I'll quit using just as soon as I finish this presentation/ attend this family reunion/get through the holiday season"—tend to stop.

STIGMA OF ADDICTION

Beyond the excuses and beyond identifying the causal links between addiction and its negative consequences, to overcome denial it is necessary to look beyond the very real possibility that addicts will be stigmatized, disgraced.

Unfortunately, it's easy—even for professionals in the field—to understand why shame sometimes prevents people from seeking the treatment they desperately need. How could it not? As I've mentioned, it's a popular misconception that addiction is not a complex physical and emotional condition but an individual failing. That view is so popular, in fact, that in a recent poll, a full 80 percent of people surveyed said that they believed that recovering addicts were discriminated against in the workforce.[2] Worse, roughly 25 percent of those same people said that, fair or not, they would be reluctant to hire someone who is in recovery. (If those around an addict feel similarly, no wonder it is so hard for a person to admit to addiction.)

In a recent survey sponsored by the National Council on Alcoholism and Drug Dependence, roughly 50 percent of those interviewed called addiction a personal weakness. And those who said that they see addiction as a disease put it into the bucket of diseases that people wind up with by making poor choices.

Being "outed" as an addict isn't difficult just because of public opinion, though. The stigma of being an addict has largely been institutionalized in the United States. The medical insurance industry often refuses to pay for alcohol or drug treatment, or else charges more for treatment than for any other diseases. In addition, often addicts are excluded from the rules that apply to pretty much everyone else. For example, state and federal agencies routinely deny much-needed welfare to anyone with prior drug convictions—even mothers needing to feed and clothe their children. And employers often fire people whom they discover to have an addiction because of their assumptions about a recovering addict's character and ability to be and remain productive. Worst of all, people who have been stigmatized often wind up feeling as if society might be right to view their alcohol and drug problems as the product of their own moral weakness.

Yet the stigma of addiction pales in comparison to the stigma of so-called mental illness. And often addicts must overcome that stigma, too, in order to begin the treatment they need. Again, it's not easy. Only about one in four Americans agrees that people are generally caring and sympathetic toward those with "mental illnesses."[3] Psychological symptoms are often seen as a mark of personal weakness. It's a common view that anxiety and depression are simply a part of life, problems that people should be able to overcome by willpower. My patients typically are quicker to admit to a drug habit than to psychiatric or emotional issues. Often they tell themselves that these issues are merely the result of substance abuse and will clear up once they get clean.

Getting past the stigma of addiction and of having an emotional issue is key to getting well, however. Not only is it imperative to get past these things in order to begin the treatment process, but the stress of hiding one's true self from family often causes other medical and social problems, including family dysfunction.

The fact is that like a physical disease, emotional and psychiatric issues are not the sufferer's "fault." We can't stress that truism enough to our patients at Creative Care. It's not a manipulation tactic. It's the truth.

HOW TO ASSESS ADDICTION

To overcome denial—beyond the excuses, and identifying the negative consequences of addiction, and accepting that the world has a skewed view of both "addicts" and the "mentally unwell"—you must surrender. You must concede that you are powerless over your addiction and be willing, if not desperate, to receive others' help.

Overcoming denial truly does require "hitting bottom," in most cases, owing in part to ego, which can become fully humbled only in the face of total personal helplessness. Also, let's face it: The prospect of surrender is often very frightening to addicts. It means giving up the one thing that, no matter what its physical or emotional toll, affords them a temporary reprieve from the hurt they feel. It is the one thing that addicts think they can control. All addicts have suffered some trauma, which typically involves a loss of control. They don't reenter this state willingly. Paradoxically, however, acknowledging loss of control is the first step toward regaining it.

Once an addict is ready for Creative Care treatment, our first step is to make sure that he or she isn't in a life-threatening situation. If he or she is neglecting such fundamental needs as food or rest, owing to depression, or acting out aggressively, or is suicidal, we need to address that situation immediately.

Once the danger is past, we screen for substance disorders while evaluating the individual's mental health. (Likewise, when we evaluate the health of someone with an obvious substance abuse issue, we screen for emotional issues at the same time. I must emphasize again that the two always go hand in hand. I can't tell you the number of people I know who struggled for years—were angry, depressed, and had even been arrested and hospitalized for bizarre behavior—without being pressed about their drug use. I've seen as many people with serious emotional issues who were given all manner of addictive barbiturates because their doctors had no idea that they were addicts.)

The assessment isn't easy. But it's not so challenging that more practitioners can't do the same screenings. The National Health Information Center, a division of the Substance Abuse and Mental Health Services (or SAMHSA, which itself is a division of the U.S. Department of Health and Human Services, www.samhsa.gov), outlines how to interview addicts on its Web site and in its print literature. Many other resources exist to help in addition to this book.

To begin the assessment, we ask people who come to us about any medication or substance they are taking. The substance abuse is sometimes more severe than the emotional issue, even if the substance abuse has exacerbated the emotional issue such that both disorders seem equally concerning.

What people are taking is important, but so is *how* they are taking it. In other words, we assess people's substance use patterns. For instance, do they tend to drink or take drugs when bored? What about when they are distraught? Do they use when alone, or when in the company of other substance abusers? Do they drink or do drugs at home or the office? As any reporter will tell you, the way to get the most information from a source is to ask open-ended questions and allow the people being interviewed to talk. Clinicians wanting to better understand an addict should follow this method.

For contextual assessment or substance use patterns, SAMHSA recommends that clinicians use these open-ended questions about symptoms to form their diagnostic criteria; this is something that we do as well.

- *When do you usually use alcohol?*
- *Who do you usually drink with? Where?*
- *What makes you think about wanting to have a drink?*
- *What is it like when you drink? How do you feel? What do you do?*
- *What do you enjoy about drinking?*
- *What are the downsides to drinking for you?*
- *What do other people think of your drinking?*

The idea is for the clinicians to assess people's expectations when they use (do they anticipate that it will ease social situations?) and their internal and external triggers for use.

SAMHSA also recommends examining criteria that can help clinicians distinguish between substance *use* and substance *abuse*, even while acknowledging that, for individuals with moderate to severe emotional issues, social drinking or drug use rarely lasts.

SAMHSA's criteria for substance *abuse* includes "maladaptive pattern of use of a substance for 12 months or more; use of substance causes problems in at least one area of function (social, interpersonal, work, family, medical, or legal)."

Its criteria for substance *use* that is evolving into substance abuse includes "maladaptive pattern of use of a substance for 12 months or more; use of the substance causes three or more of the following: tolerance, withdrawal, uses more than planned or for more time than intended, desire to cut down, reduces other activities to use, uses despite problems (social, interpersonal, work, family, medical, or legal)."

STABILIZING ADDICTS

It is also important to understand how the substance use impacts the addicts. In other words, do they feel better or worse for using? Does drug or alcohol use ameliorate stress or otherwise confer positive things, such as better sleep? Alternately, what's the downside?

Sometimes it's difficult for individuals to recount their feelings and use patterns precisely through a straightforward interview, so we ask people to verbally walk us through a typical day in their lives, from the time they awake until they go to sleep. We want to know where they go, whom they see, and where they turn for alcohol and/or drugs.

Because substance abuse and emotional issues often conspire to produce fantastic rationalizations, we also always question the veracity of this day-in-the-life accounting (though even the most outlandish stories can offer helpful insights into a person).

Also, because not everyone is going to confess the full extent of their substance abuse, we always get the "full picture" by interviewing family members, friends, and sometimes even coworkers. And trust me, many times their accounts differ dramatically from the individual's own narrative.

Individuals with severe issues tend to lead rather isolated existences, so it's often important to turn where possible to hospital records and urine drug screens for accurate information. (Individuals who are most resistant to taking such tests typically are abusing some sort of substance.)

Once we have a picture of the degree of substance abuse we're facing, the next step is convincing the addicts that it is imperative that they eliminate all drug or alcohol use. To produce an accurate diagnosis, abstinence isn't merely helpful—it's a requirement. Furthermore, the sooner people embrace abstinence, the sooner their emotional issues will start to improve. (One hundred percent of the time, substance abuse intensifies and worsens emotional problems.)

Convincing addicts to stop their behavior can be exceedingly challenging. People often blame the outcome of their addicted behavior—broken relationships, lost jobs—for why they use as much as they do; in their eyes, they are hapless victims who are not accountable for what befalls them.

Even those individuals who come to recognize the toll of their substance-fueled behavior often believe that they can help themselves through sheer willpower.

Some clinicians indulge this fantasy, too. They support these people's efforts, knowing full well that they will almost always fail to save themselves on their own. (Such clinicians apparently hope that the addicts will return when they are truly ready. They complicitly support their patients' judgment on the basis that "it's their life.")

While clinicians might encourage these addicts to enter 12 Step treatment programs, they don't push; these clinicians merely let patients know that they are there if and when patients want to engage in formal treatment.

I am not passing judgment on this attitude. Certainly I recognize that it is not possible to engage every person in his or her own treatment. But the people we treat usually have proven time and again that they do not have the resources to help themselves—that it isn't a matter of willpower. Often these people do not understand what is wrong or why they are in so much pain.

For these reasons, I believe that it's crucial to shine a light on the gravity of the situation and to expose the contradictions in patients' lives. It's crucial to break down their defenses and, if they try to quit treatment, to do everything possible to highlight for them that they could be making a life-threatening mistake. (A caveat here: Although every individual's defenses can be broken down, clinicians must decide how, and at what pace, to do so on a case-by-case basis. Confronting people too vigorously early in the treatment process can heighten their anxiety, which can worsen their emotional state. It's best to hold back on the most emotionally charged material until patients are better able to cope with it.)

It's also very important to note that even those who *can* be convinced of the need for abstinence often fall off the wagon— repeatedly. (Remember, we're talking about chronic conditions.) This is the reason we continually assess the people who come to us. Just because the information we gather initially from patients, family, and drug tests may point to certain conclusions does not mean that those conclusions will forever remain accurate. Sometimes patients start using again after they leave us; sometimes a psychiatric symptom emerges—or vanishes—after months of sobriety. Time to observe is absolutely essential, and information must be culled constantly to stay ahead of the issues.

ADDICTION IN MENTAL HEALTH SETTINGS

Once we have an accurate picture of people's drug use and we've convinced them to try abstinence, unlike most addiction treatment facilities, we start their psychological and/or psychiatric treatment.

Screening for emotional issues in those with substance issues is different from a straightforward addiction evaluation. Indeed, the screening process is different at addiction treatment facilities and at mental health facilities.

For individuals who are entering mental health treatment facilities—where, because the primary focus is not on addiction, people likely will not come clean about the degree of their substance abuse—some organizations, including SAMHSA, recommend employing the 18-question survey known as the Dartmouth Assessment of Lifestyle (DALI).[4]

DALI's authors developed the survey in 1998 after examining the diagnoses of substance use disorder for 247 patients admitted to a state hospital, and then using logistic regression to select the best items from ten screening instruments. They constructed their test and tried it out on 73 admitted patients. DALI is just one survey that helps measure substance abuse disorders in individuals with severe emotional issues. Its benefit is that it is simple to use, and it is particularly helpful in the early stages of treatment—before patient and clinician have established enough trust and rapport for the patient to know he or she can speak frankly and provide accurate information.

Most of the DALI questions can be answered with a yes or no. For others, test takers choose a number that helps put some of their habits and feelings into perspective. Because the numerical scores assigned to questions would be meaningless to most readers, I am omitting them. More important in our context are the questions themselves.

1. *Do you wear seatbelts while riding in the car?*
2. *How many cigarettes do you smoke each day?*
3. *Have you tried to stop smoking cigarettes?*
4. *Do you control your diet for total calories (amount you eat)?*
5. *How much would you say you spent during the past six months on alcohol?*
6. *How many drinks can you hold without passing out? [Interviewer note: If patient does not know, ask "How many do you think it would take?"]*
7. *Have close friends or relatives worried or complained about your drinking in the past six months?*
8. *Have you ever attended a meeting of Alcoholics Anonymous (AA) because of your drinking?*
9. *Do you sometimes take a drink in the morning?*
10. *How long was your last period of voluntary abstinence from alcohol? (or "most recent period when you chose not to drink.") [Interviewer note: two weeks or more equals a month. Exclude periods of incarceration or hospitalization.]*
11. *How many months ago did this abstinence end for alcohol? (or "when did you start drinking?)*

12. *Have you used marijuana in the past six months?*

13. *Have you lost a job because of marijuana use?*

14. *How much would you say you spent in the past six months on marijuana?*

15. *How troubled or bothered have you been in the past six months by marijuana problems?*

16. *Has cocaine abuse created problems between you and your spouse or your parents?*

17. *How long was your last period of voluntary abstinence from cocaine? (or "most recent period when you chose not to use?") [Interviewer note: two weeks or more equals a month. Exclude periods of incarceration or hospitalization.]*

18. *Do you ever use cocaine when you're in a bad mood?*

UNDERSTANDING THE PROGNOSIS

Once an individual in a mental health setting is diagnosed as having substance abuse issues, what's next? At Creative Care, we start by emphasizing several points to help patients and their family better understand the situation, the most important of which is that addiction is hardly rare in psychiatric settings. Many people with emotional issues (severe or less so) have substance abuse problems as well.

I always underscore, too, that both emotional issues and addiction issues *can* be treated and resolved. The fact that both are chronic and lifelong does not mean that they are untreatable or that the individuals they impact are in hopeless situations. Quite the opposite is true. Both issues can be managed with the appropriate treatment, which typically involves support groups and therapy and, when warranted by a mental health condition, daily medication.

Now, not every treatment process or combination of therapy and/or medication will look the same. (Some people will benefit more than others from the support of peer groups, for example. Some people will move through the phases of recovery—from stabilization, to treatment, to ongoing rehabilitation—more quickly than will others.)

Every course of treatment must be adapted to the meet the needs of the unique individual in need of help.

Given the appropriate tools, though, individuals can regain their sense of self-worth, self-love, and, as important, purpose.

ADDICTION IN ALCOHOL AND DRUG TREATMENT SETTINGS

Screening for emotional issues at an addiction treatment facility like the Betty Ford Clinic is somewhat different and can be more challenging. The challenge, as I've discussed, is that the substance abuse is usually so severe that it's difficult to distinguish which symptoms are a result of the addiction and which are related to a potential emotional issue.

Though we often see people who present an array of emotional issues in addiction treatment settings, often patients poorly understand those issues, if they recognize them at all. (Obviously, people might be aware that they are despairing, say, but they might assign those feelings to circumstances, when in fact a biochemical disorder is causing shifts in their moods.)

A growing number of researchers are beginning to argue that despite historical and recent assumptions to the contrary, there is little evidence that natural boundaries separate most currently recognized mental disorders. They believe that variation in symptoms is continuous, and so they question the validity of contemporary classifications.

Neither side is fully right or wrong, in my view. In the meantime, the categories offer strong guidance; generally it is found that people with close approximations to a condition or conditions listed in the *Diagnostic and Statistical Manual of Mental Disorders (DSM)*[5] have that particular disorder.

Either way, once a course of action has been identified, the psychological/psychiatric piece of treatment should begin conservatively, through encouragement, support, and understanding. Introducing therapy (both individual and/or group, depending on the person's comfort level) as early into the process as possible is also key.

ONCE YOU RECOGNIZE ADDICTION

Addicts face a tough uphill battle. Among other things, there's evidence that substance abuse leads to worsening emotional issues and, later, to terrible external outcomes, including health problems, family issues, financial struggles, homelessness, and even, potentially, death. In short, the consequences of not treating addiction can be grave.

Screening can be challenging, as well.

Different treatments are effective at different stages. What works at the outset of treatment differs dramatically from what works later, during active treatment. What works during active treatment also differs from what works in the final, unending stage of treatment: the stage of managing and sustaining rehabilitation. By getting to know and understand the unique characteristics of an individual's disorders and identifying the appropriate stage of treatment, it is possible to marry the best possible course of treatment with someone's issues, goals, and readiness to embrace change.

Fortunately, we have recognized that the more time that our staff and our patients spend together, the greater the trust between them, and that's when the real breakthroughs can happen: when an individual feels safe enough to speak candidly about issues and enlist the help of others who are doing what they can to make that person well.

Again, the first step—and perhaps the hardest one—is getting past denial. It is also the first step toward survival.

The Hidden Roots of Addiction

*T*HERE IS NO SINGLE cause of addiction. Both your genes and the environment you come from play pivotal roles. But emotional and psychiatric issues also contribute to shaping a person's compulsive behavior and his inclination to get attached to mind-altering substances.

The emotional issues that cause addiction often are connected with unprocessed trauma, such as experiencing or witnessing physical or emotional violence, or sexual abuse. This trauma gives rise to depression, anxiety, anger, and other negative feelings, which drive people to self-medicate with alcohol and drugs. Up to two-thirds of both men and women who have undergone substance abuse treatment say they have suffered from childhood abuse or neglect.[1] Since this data relies on self-reporting, the actual number is probably even higher. In my professional experience, nearly every addicted patient has suffered an emotional trauma. And when you experience a trauma, it can trigger any predisposition you might have toward addiction.

I don't claim that addicts are necessarily more troubled than nonaddicts. Many of us struggle with emotional issues. I also don't mean to intimate that every addict you know was abused at some point in childhood, since most certainly that is not the case. But I will tell you that in my experience, many of our patients play out traumatic issues—often deeply buried and often deriving from their family of origin—through addiction.

The emotional issues that lead to addiction often are related to unprocessed trauma, such as experiencing or witnessing physical or emotional violence, or sexual abuse.

Within the last couple of years, for example, Creative Care has had two patients who were addicted to alcohol and had no idea of the extent to which of their addictions derived from childhood traumas.

As it happens, Alastair and John had the same outward characteristics. Both were successful businessmen, both were high-functioning alcoholics, and both were afraid of being "present." (In other words, both reacted very poorly to the roughly two hours of downtime each day at our treatment center, during which patients are to sit by themselves and introspect in a safe place.)

When not actively engaged, Alastair carried around armfuls of papers: the business section of the day's newspaper, accounting ledgers, and notes on work-related ideas that he was brainstorming and intended to implement once he was back at work. Similarly, John constantly needed distractions and aggressively sought out conversations with other patients, with our staff, with delivery persons; without them, he would have panic attacks.

Alastair had a contentious relationship with his children. They saw him as angry and detached. He, who had made it possible for them to have every worldly good, saw them as spoiled, and he resented them for it. John didn't have children, but he tried to control his fourth wife, who said that within their home, as with John's work, everything was a power struggle.

Certainly, a huge problem in the lives of both men was alcohol, which no doubt exacerbated their bad behavior within their own families. But alcohol itself wasn't the root problem. On the contrary, both men were rendered emotionally inaccessible by their childhoods, which were painful periods for each of them.

Alastair's biological mother had given him up when he was born, and due to health issues he lived in an incubator for four weeks until his adoptive parents came to claim him. Worse, his adoptive parents divorced when he was a young teenager, and their custody battle involved who *had* to take him, not who wanted to have him. Little wonder that he later married a woman—the mother of his children—who was ambivalent toward him.

John, meanwhile, also suffered a serious attachment injury. At the age of 12, a time when he was rebelling against his parents, his father dropped him off at a mental institution. Neither parent saw John again until they picked him up several months later.

Unfortunately, the damage had been done. Until coming to Creative Care, both men spent their lives fearing abandonment. For example, that John treated his wife harshly—and the three wives who preceded her—didn't surprise me; he was terrified of caring too much and then being left alone.

Only by understanding the genesis of their emotional issues and their severity could both men, who had been in and out of a number of treatment facilities, finally realize why they were compelled to drink—and how to stop.

UNPROCESSED TRAUMA

The emotional issues that cause addiction are often connected with unprocessed trauma. Yet a trauma can be different things to different people. Alastair and John endured specific, lasting upsets—the incubator, the custody battle, being taken to a mental institution for behaving badly—but plenty of people walk around with unprocessed traumas that are far more amorphous: damage by parents who consistently undermined their child because of their own unresolved emotional issues, or divorced parents who refused to share custody. The scenarios are many. The point is that unprocessed traumas don't always boil down to outright abuse.

Again, sometimes it's easier to understand people when you hear their stories directly, so let me introduce you to another former patient of Creative Care: Julia.

Like Andrew and so many of our patients, Julia did not arrive displaying the superficial signs of addiction.

Trauma can affect different people in different ways.

JULIA'S STORY

On the surface, Julia looks like any attractive, self-confident woman you might see on the street. A tall, slender 27-year-old with a curtain of long blond hair and bright green eyes, she is pretty and effervescent, the youngest of four children.

Indeed, when Julia first arrived at Creative Care, her stories matched her sunny disposition. She told us that her upbringing was very happy. She and her siblings had the usual trappings of an upper-middle-class family: access to good private schools, nice cars, family vacations, and an array of furry friends, including guinea pigs, hamsters, parakeets, and cats.

She said that she was close to her brother and two sisters, the oldest of whom is ten years older than Julia, and that it wasn't her parents' fault that she'd become an addict.

Then the real story began to take shape. Julia slowly began to admit that though she was popular and well liked, she had very dark moments, and she coped with them by becoming a bulimic and by turning to alcohol. In Julia's own words,

> I starting using alcohol at 15, on weekends. I was at that age when kids experiment, and like most kids, I found that alcohol made it easier to go to parties. I wasn't as self-conscious or nervous when I had a little bit of a buzz.
>
> Around the same time, I started throwing up food on occasion after a friend first introduced me to the concept in an abstract way. "Eat whatever you want, then make yourself throw up so that you don't gain any weight." I thought it sounded brilliant. I didn't gorge myself constantly, but I would sometimes eat a sleeve or two of Oreos or a bag of potato chips when I knew my privacy was assured, then I'd gag myself after.
>
> As for the alcohol, I drank your standard things: mostly beer, sometimes liquor stolen from my parents' or my friends' parents' liquor cabinets. On very rare occasions, when it was offered to us, usually at parties, my girlfriends and I would also do cocaine and LSD. That was really exotic for us. It was all social use.
>
> I was fine throughout high school. Then I made the decision not to go to college right away. I really wanted to travel instead. So I did that for a couple of years, traveling through-out Europe mostly.

When I returned, though, I became really depressed about the fact that I had no direction and was living in my parents' home again while all of my friends were in college, doing more interesting things. I just suddenly felt, I don't know, less than.... Not good enough. And I started to realize that I'd always felt that way. So I started to drink to numb that frustration.

At first, it was not a big deal; I partied. I picked up new friends, other people who weren't in college, who were working.

But within four months of her return to New York, Julia, who'd begun working as a job recruiter, was drinking daily.

I began to enjoy the ritual of it, and the way it made me feel — and not feel. I wasn't just eager to hit the bars to drink. I was buying bottles at the liquor store and hiding them everywhere in my bedroom: under my bed, in my closet, in my drawers. That feeling of liquor, warming me, protecting me, loosening my inhibitions, quickly became all that mattered.

I wasn't sure how it had happened, but getting high, getting drunk, was all I could think about. I spent time strategizing how to plan my schedule so that I could take off stretches of work and spend two or three days alone in my parents' home, where I was still living, and just use.

But I still worked. I was still the good daughter. I wasn't sloppy in front of anyone; it was my own little, harmless secret. No one knew, or needed to know, that I was growing totally paranoid at the time, peering out of my window, imagining paratroopers were tapping on it. No one knew I wasn't sleeping; no one knew I was either not eating or, depending on the moment, eating and throwing up.

Julia thought she was maintaining, but it was becoming apparent, at least to her father, that something was very wrong.

> I would work out like crazy. I'd get high and do Tae Bo. I'd get drunk, then eat whatever I could get my hands on to soak up the alcohol, then I'd make myself barf up everything so I wouldn't get fat. Even half out of my mind, I was worried about my appearance, and it was very important to me to stay thin. It wasn't always junk food, either. Sometimes I'd throw up a perfectly normal, healthy meal. Even when I started to realize that I was probably no longer in "normal" territory, I had a hard time controlling myself.
>
> I remember working out in my parents' front yard at 11 at night. My dad, who was very disciplined and was always in bed by 10, came out of the house and asked me with this really horrified look on his face: "What are you doing?" I'll never forget the concern in his eyes.

Julia didn't realize that her chemical dependency and eating disorder were connected.

> Around that time, the coke had become especially bad. I went from casually using to snorting lines in my bedroom closet. I'd stay up until 1 o'clock or 2, then pretend to sleep. As soon as I heard that everyone had left the house in the morning, I was doing another line.
>
> It just became worse and worse. Every morning, I was literally reaching for a bottle of vodka underneath my bed to get the shakes off. My sheets were drenched in sweat. I had horrible anxiety. I was crying myself to sleep every night. My friends all ditched me because I'd flaked on them one too many times.

Nearly a year after Julia moved back in with her parents, her father was diagnosed with pancreatic cancer and was admitted to the hospital almost immediately. In the throes of addiction, Julia did the unthinkable: She stole money from his hospital room nightstand so that she could buy cocaine. Three weeks later, he passed away.

> *After my father's death, the coke stopped but the alcohol soared. I was in a miserable place. I thought he died so I could live, so I tried to be functional. I was still working as a recruiter. But I was binge drinking, going out to clubs, gorging myself and throwing up. I was angry and depressed, and everything was made worse by push-pull relationship I was in with a boyfriend, who was a cheat, something I tried to ignore. I'd go through a fifth of vodka before he picked me up, so at the dinner table, I'd be drunk after one or two drinks, and become really giggly or argumentative, depending on the tone of the evening. When we eventually broke up, I started drinking even more heavily.*
>
> *For the longest time, my mother had no idea; alcoholics are great actors. And maybe she was in denial, having lived through her experience with her parents [who were also alcoholics]. She didn't know that I was dying and miserable and soulless and spiritless and hopeless on the inside.*

Eventually that same year, Julia's mother found her slumped over her desktop computer, sobbing. After the first frank conversation that the two had had in a very long time and with Julia's consent, the two began to investigate treatment options.

> *I first went into treatment in Laguna Beach, California. I lasted three weeks. The program didn't resonate at all because*

I still hadn't hit rock bottom. In fact, I got out on Christmas Day, which is my birthday, and immediately started celebrating by heading to the closest liquor store, picking up a bottle of champagne, and spending the rest of the day drinking.

Somehow I survived for several months more in that state, when I went in for help at another residential facility in Burbank. That was pretty hard core. The facility I'd entered really believes in breaking you down, including having you scrub toilets, but it's a great program and I spent a month there and I did well.

Julia did so well, she thought that when she was urged to live in a sober living group home—which is what we advocate, as well, because it's very challenging to avoid cues to drink in those first months of recovery—she said no.

I said no, I'm fine, I'm great. Well, that lasted a week and a half. I thought I'd surrendered when I was there, but I still hadn't. Though I knew logically what I needed to do, I still drove to the store one afternoon in the middle of a weekday, bought another bottle of champagne, and drank it.

I still had my job—my boss had been very supportive of me, telling me she'd hold my position while I was in rehab—but when I was interviewing job candidates later that same afternoon, they knew what was up. They were like: You are supposed to be helping me? That's a laugh.

Not long after that, I was drunk one afternoon while driving—again—and pulled over to the side of the road not far from my parents' home and called a friend to come and pick me up. He came but instead of driving me anywhere, he sort of took advantage of me [sexually] in the back of the car. It wasn't rape. I knew what was happening and allowed it, but I was repulsed by myself for it and afterward I was a wreck because I'm not that girl. So I went home, sat my mother down, and said, "I don't want to die." That's when we found Creative Care.

Like many of our patients, Julia wasn't exactly happy when she first arrived at our door. Though she knew it was necessary, she wasn't eager to give up the bottle. She was angry with herself for already relapsing twice. And her mother had to mortgage her house to pay for Julia's treatment. She was filled with self-loathing.

What Julia learned at Creative Care was why: why she thought so little of herself, why she abused herself as she did, and why she allowed others to abuse her.

It wasn't some buried memory. It wasn't even a struggle that she herself was embroiled in. She learned that her parents' strained marital relationship had caused her enduring childhood trauma. She realized that though there were no physical fights or even screaming matches, she had absorbed some difficult things. Specifically, throughout her childhood, she saw her stern father, a former military man who rarely showed his emotions, and her mother, damaged by alcoholic parents and in need of constant reassurance, in what was a loveless marriage. The couple even told their children, both directly and indirectly, that they stayed together purely for their sakes.

Such breakthroughs came slowly but surely in the group therapy sessions that our patients participate in every morning and afternoon, as well as in Julia's one-on-one meetings with the primary psychiatrist assigned to her. (All of our patients participate in at least as much therapy as Julia.) She talked about her family, and she talked about how easy it was to control her food as a way to control her emotions, and she continued to talk and talk and within a few weeks, she began to turn a corner.

Upsetting as it was for her to reconcile herself to the damage that growing up in such an environment caused her, Julia's intensive therapy sessions helped her to realize how her parents' relationship influenced how she felt about herself and why she entered the relationships that she did, including the one with the ex-boyfriend who cheated on her.

She also began to forgive herself for the pain she had caused everyone as she came to understand that many people with unresolved traumas learn to "medicate" themselves.

Equally as important, Julia learned for the first time in many years how to live sober. At the beginning of her stay at Creative Care she took a short course of naltrexone (marketed as Depade and Vivitrol), a medication that offers addicts a short-term crutch and that, when used in concert with psychosocial therapies for alcohol-dependent or alcohol-abusing patients, can drastically ease dependence. She also worked closely with what we call a "secondary" counselor, who works with each patient expressly on 12 Step recovery issues, and attended 12 Step meetings every evening, as do all of our patients at Creative Care. Julia, also like all of our patients, was given a temporary sponsor. And Julia's mother was enlisted.

When you put everything together, it's a very comprehensive approach. Still, I'll tell you what made all the difference: the magic with Julia is that she was able to give up control in order to obtain true control. The patient who gets better is the one who participates in the process and anticipates the things that trigger their addiction (bars, friends, certain thoughts) and works through them. It was the key in Julia's case, and it's the key to recovery every time: an addict who becomes interested in their own recovery, who recognizes his or her limitations—recognizes that the problem is bigger than him or her and consequently takes direction—and who decides that it's time to turn things around.

Julia was always driving the bus, so to speak. She refused to sit in the back. She was always very willful and opinionated about what worked for her and what didn't, but she finally realized the need to trust us, rather than follow her own instincts and do things her own way, and it saved her.

Today she has been sober for three years, and she works to transition addicts into sober living situations. And she is happy.

> *I have new girlfriends and I've reconnected with old girl-friends. I'm active in AA, attending three to five meetings a week. My ties with my family have never been stronger. In fact, my sisters and brother ask me for emotional advice now.*

Most important, Julia has learned to love and accept herself, no matter how she is feeling.

> *Today, if I'm in a crap pile, I think about what I'm thankful for. I still don't have the college degree that I'd like. I'm not happy with where I am financially. But everything is easier sober, and now I know that sometimes you just have to roll through it and go to bed. I know that tomorrow's a new day.*

EMOTIONAL TRAUMA

All addicts have emotional and psychiatric issues that play a much greater role in their lives than even they realize—if they realize it at all.

> *Often the emotional issues that cause addiction are connected with unprocessed trauma, which give rise to feelings like depression and anger and self-loathing.*

Trauma is a powerful word, of course. When it's used on television, it's often in the context of physical violence or sexual abuse or murder. But many people are affected by many different kinds of traumas, and they are affected differently by what they experience.

Narrowly defined, trauma is an event or a series of events that compromise an individual's sense of safety and sanity. The classic root cause of trauma is being the subject of sexual or physical violence, but trauma can also include witnessing such events as a child or even perpetrating them.

Any situation that makes a person feel helpless can result in a trauma.

Abandonment is a common expression of a helpless state. John and Alastair both had attachment issues without recognizing them. Meanwhile, Andrew hated himself without realizing why. He didn't understand he had conjured up expectations of himself that he then failed to live up to. He wasn't aware of the degree to which he lived in the shadow of a father whom he worried—wrongly, as he would much later realize—didn't love him very much.

It bears repeating: Nearly 66 percent of addicts who come to treatment facilities say that they've suffered from childhood abuse or neglect. Likely closer to 100 percent have been victims of at least one trauma that has defined who they have become.

It is vital to uncover these traumas and to address them. Not doing so almost guarantees that an addict will relapse. As the stories of both Julia and Andrew have underscored, if underlying emotional issues are not addressed within the safe, nurturing confines of a treatment facility, they will most assuredly become a problem again for the addict when he or she returns to the outside world.

6

~
ℰ

The Role Environment
Plays in Addiction

DESPITE POPULAR BELIEF, ONLY a small percentage of people who try drugs get hooked. Drugs themselves are not the sole cause of addiction. So why do some people develop addictions while others do not?

Although no one has identified a specific gene for alcoholism, adoption and twin studies indicate that genes play a role in vulnerability to alcoholism.[1] But like cardiovascular disease, genes alone don't dictate whether you'll develop alcohol or drug addiction. In fact, I believe strongly that environmental influences—from family, to friends, to schools, to the community one lives in—are even more significant in determining who are most at risk of becoming addicts. Even geography can play a role.

Genes are not a sole deciding factor in whether you'll develop alcohol or drug addiction, but studies indicate that they play a part in certain people becoming vulnerable to alcoholism.

FAMILY FACTOR

In my experience, factors associated with our family of origin have the strongest environmental impact on the way we view and use both drugs and alcohol. The inescapable fact is that children's environment—good or bad—largely informs who they become.

This is absolutely not to say that adult children of alcoholics will turn out to be bad people, or even alcoholics themselves. But alcoholism within the home often influences people to drink as adults. After all, home and family form the foundation of what a child deems normal or acceptable. Very often light-drinking parents produce light-drinking children and parents who drink heavily have children who also drink heavily—unless they react against their parents' heavy drinking and abstain. We see that, too. In fact, another common outcome is that children drink little or not at all in reaction to their parents' behavior and the problems associated with it.

There are yet other ways in which family impacts the individual. For example, people born to families that later see a parent leave—or, in worst cases, both parents—are more prone to having emotional issues and becoming entangled in drugs and alcohol than people born into families that remain happily intact. With divorce affecting half of all marriages and another fraction staying together for the children, that is a high number.[2]

There is also a higher risk of having emotional issues for children whose parents stay together but are constantly at one another's throats or are never home. Both scenarios tend to stress children as well as give them more freedom than they can handle. That freedom often translates into greater susceptibility to peer pressure.

Unfortunately, given U.S. divorce rates, even kids living with a parent and stepparent or other nonrelative have a slightly higher risk of using alcohol and drugs than kids living with both of their natural parents, according to a major study conducted by the U.S. Department of Health and Human Services in 1997. (The good news: If the same degree of social support and communication found in families with both natural parents is provided to children living with stepparents or nonrelatives, the disparity vanishes.)

As if this weren't gloomy enough news, let me explain how some families physically create lasting challenges for their children.

According to research published by the National Institutes of Health (NIH), the primary federal agency for conducting and supporting medical research, environmental factors associated with their parents' drinking very often affect the *brains* of children who become alcohol dependent later in life.

Think about that for a moment. As you may know, children of alcoholics are known to have a greater risk for alcohol dependence. Sometimes they are born with fetal alcohol syndrome. And as I mentioned in chapter 2, researchers now believe that some children whose mothers who drank during their pregnancy enter the world with slightly altered brain chemistry, which can impact the way that they behave, including making them less inhibited.

Now researchers strongly suspect that brain growth among alcoholics with a family history of alcoholism or heavy drinking is stunted *after they are born*. How? Why? Children of addicts often experience not only adverse psychological effects from unstable relationships within the home but also biological effects, including poor diet.[3]

The sad reality is that many children of alcoholics have to fend for themselves. A dear friend of mine remembers, at age four, preparing bowls of cereal for himself for breakfast, lunch, and dinner—always without milk, which was never in the refrigerator—because his mother was suffering from severe depression and alcoholism and sometimes locked herself in her dark bedroom for days.

The fact that brain growth can be impacted by one's environment is a frightening assertion to be sure. Indeed, to back up their findings that tie brain diminution to alcohol after a child has been born, the researchers used magnetic resonance imaging (MRI) techniques to measure the volume of the cranium—the part of the skull that encapsulates the brain—in a group of people who were being treated for alcohol addiction. (The intracranial volume, or ICV, is determined by the growth of the skull, which hits its maximum size during puberty and remains the same size for the rest of a person's life.)

What they found was that, on average, the ICV of the adult children of alcoholics was roughly 4 percent smaller than the ICV of individuals without alcoholic parents. (It didn't matter how much the adult children themselves drank.) The researchers also discovered that the adult children of alcoholics had lower IQ scores than those without alcoholic parents—roughly 5.7 points lower on average.

Children of addicts often experience not only adverse psychological effects from unstable relationships within the home but also physical effects.

According to the NIH study, a possible implication of the findings is that the increased risk for alcoholism among children of alcoholics may be due to a genetic or environmental effect, or both. The study's lead author, Daniel Hommer, M.D., explained it in this way: "Although ICV is known to be influenced primarily by genetic factors, many studies have found that living in an enriched environment promotes central nervous system growth and development. It seems likely that alcoholics, in general, are raised in less than optimal environments and thus that genetics and environment both contribute to the smaller ICV observed in family history positive alcoholics."

MARRIAGE FACTOR

It is not only your family of origin that can have an enormous environmental impact on your use of drugs and alcohol. The family that you form as an adult is another strong environmental influence.

I can't tell you how many addicts who are married to addicts have come to Creative Care. As the old adage goes, like marries like. In other words, people often marry people who are more similar to them than not. They gravitate to people who come from the same socioeconomic or cultural or educational background. They often choose people who have lived in the same places or experienced many of the same things. In addition, people tend to marry people with personalities similar to their own. Overachievers often wed other overachievers, for example, or depressed individuals wed individuals who themselves struggle to find happiness.

Not surprisingly, people at risk of becoming alcoholics tend to marry individuals who are also at risk, sometimes because their backgrounds and upbringing (and parents) were so alike.

The most interesting thing about these addict couples is the positive impact that coming together can have. I'm not referring to various findings that married couples live longer, happier lives than their single counterparts. I'm telling you what I have seen firsthand: Married alcoholics often react to one another by stopping drinking.

Research supports what I have experienced anecdotally. For example, researchers from Washington University and the Queensland Institute of Medical Research in Brisbane, Australia, recently published their study of roughly 6,000 Australian twins born between 1902 and 1964 and those twins' spouses.[4] After accounting statistically for the fact that people tend to marry similar people, the researchers observed that one partner's problem drinking tended to reduce the likelihood that the other would also become or remain a problem drinker. (One researcher postulated that one spouse might have to take greater responsibility for the couple's children, although the theories behind why one partner drank less as the other drank more were inconclusive.)

Divorcing a spouse can be another powerful environmental determinant in who does and does not develop an addiction. For one thing, newly separated and divorced people are more likely than their married counterparts to spend time at bars, restaurants, and other places where people come together to socialize and, invariably, to drink. After all, even if they have less disposable income than they did as part of a married couple, they have more leisure time.

Often there are also psychiatric consequences when marriages break down, including anxiety disorders and depression, which, as I've explained, often go hand in hand with alcoholism. Little wonder that the strong association between divorce and subsequent ill health, both physical and mental, has led marriage proponents to argue that reducing divorce rates would vastly improve public health.

PEERS AND COMMUNITY

Other environmental influences sway individuals who may already be at risk of developing an addiction to drugs or alcohol. People's connection with the community in which they live plays a part in their likelihood of abusing drugs. The more active they are—and the less isolated—the better their chances of leading a balanced, healthy lifestyle.

Yet the community itself is also commonly an actor in the story. Growing up in a neighborhood where there's nothing to attach to—no sports or after-school programs to be a part of, no mentors to watch over and inspire and organize the community's children—can be very detrimental. Also elevating risk are extreme economic deprivation, high rates of transience within a community (which sometimes accounts for why there is little to attach to, and few mentors), and social disorganization, meaning that not only do at-risk youth have no after-school programs but there are few other programs in which they can engage.

Friends who drink or abuse alcohol can be influential, particularly when children do not have a strong foundation at home. Not all children are susceptible to peer pressure, of course. But many are, and a good percentage of those who succumb do so because they're depressed, have attention deficit disorder, or suffer from another psychological issue. Others succumb because their peers have rejected them; they use alcohol or drugs to cope with the alienation they feel.

Not last, and perhaps most tragically, physical and sexual abuse play an enormous environmental role in the lives of many people who become addicts. Kids and teenagers who have been sexually abused suffer horrible psychological problems, both at the time the abuse occurs and throughout their lives. Some of these problems include, in the short term, depression, anxiety, guilt, fear, and withdrawal.[5] But the negative effects of child sexual abuse can torment someone well into adulthood. Many adults who were victimized as children develop severe depression as well as high levels of anxiety. As adults, they address these issues with even more self-destructive behavior, including becoming alcoholics and drug abusers.

The fact that an environment of childhood abuse—sexual, physical, or, in worst cases, both—can produce adult alcoholics with psychiatric issues is becoming increasingly better documented.

A 2004 study, for example, concluded that compared with other environmental risk factors, childhood sexual and physical abuse contributed to the coexisting disorders of anxiety and alcoholism. Researchers in Amsterdam documented that abuse was a particularly significant factor in alcoholics who suffer from agoraphobia and posttraumatic stress disorder. The study also found that "more severe and intrusive forms of early sexual abuse as well as early multiple traumas are associated with a more complex symptom constellation that includes chronic mood disorder and inclination to suicide."[6]

CONCLUSION

When I say that the nature of our addiction is framed by our environment, I am really talking about the social context: the people to whom we connect and the spaces we inhabit. What kind of pressures do they exert on us?

The challenge in tracing the source of an emotional trauma is that it is easy for its impact to blend into the surroundings. The question is: Does a trauma get buried because it is too terrible to face? Or does an unpleasant event assume outsize importance in our psyches, forcing the brain to work extra hard to eclipse it and resulting in trauma?

When thinking about the causes of addiction—either yours or your loved one's—think about the possible sources of trauma that may be hidden in the deep recesses of memory.

7

How the Brain Changes with Addiction

WHILE ALCOHOLISM IS EASY enough to identify once you take a hard look, and although it has a predictably ruinous course if it is not addressed, its physical foundation was a complete enigma for decades.

No longer. Far more work needs to be done, but over the past decade, researchers have made tremendous strides toward identifying the physical culprits involved in alcoholism, largely by using advanced technology such as MRI scans. Their work has better enabled them to understand how the brain of an addict differs from that of a nonaddict as well as how alcohol interacts with the body.

For example, it's long been known that men and women become addicted to alcohol at different rates, with women succumbing to alcohol much more quickly. There have also long been theories as to why this is true; reasons offered include the facts that women are smaller and they have less water weight to dilute alcohol's effect.

Both suppositions are accurate to a degree, but researchers have learned another reason why women tend to get drunk more quickly and sometimes fall onto a faster track to alcoholism: They metabolize alcohol much more slowly than men. The reason? Women have fewer stomach enzymes, including an enzyme in the stomach lining called alcohol dehydrogenase (ADH), which is the first to tackle the ethanol in liquor.

The smaller amount of ADH in a woman's system allows more pure ethanol to enter her bloodstream. She thus becomes high on the same amount of alcohol that her male counterpart has had to drink, while he experiences little to no effect. The outcome is that some women feel intoxicated so quickly that they stop drinking. For others, however, the outcome is the polar opposite: They become attached to the quick high that they derive from drinking and try to recreate the experience. (I've seen the comparison made before to diabetes, and it's an apt analogy. Just as some people are unable to process sugar quickly enough, women can't process alcohol very effectively, either. Diabetes is a good analogy for another reason: Like alcoholism, it is chronic, and afflicted individuals grow worse over time.)

THE BRAIN

Today the brain can be analyzed every which way through magnetic resonance imaging (MRI), which has provided scientists with a better understanding of the physical origins of addiction.

One area of ongoing interest is the prefrontal cortex, an analytical part of the brain that helps us with decision making. The prefrontal cortex is also what allows rational thought to override impulsive behavior.

Over the years, a lot of research has shown that adults with alcoholism generally have smaller brain sizes than nonalcoholics. Newer research has discovered something potentially more surprising. In one particular study several years ago, researchers used MRI scans to measure several parts of the brain for 14 teenagers with addiction issues and 28 teenagers from similar socioeconomic and geographic backgrounds who were known to not have addiction issues.[1] All of the youngsters were between 13 and 17 years of age. The addicted teens were recruited from substance abuse treatment programs and had coexisting mental health issues, while the others were recruited through a newspaper ad.

What the researchers found was that the teens with drinking and drug problems and mental disorders had smaller prefrontal cortexes, just like adult alcoholics. The scientists involved with the study hypothesized that with less white matter in the prefrontal cortex, the adolescents' ability to make complex decisions is compromised. That includes decisions about when to give in to urges and contemplating the consequences of one's actions.

Unfortunately, not much can be done with the findings at this point. What no one knows yet—and what will be a powerful finding one day—is whether individuals born with a smaller prefrontal cortex are more vulnerable to alcohol and drug addiction, or whether individuals, through early-onset alcohol and drug abuse, stunt their own brain growth. In short, as with many aspects of addiction, researchers continue to struggle with what part of the puzzle comes first.

ROLE OF NEUROTRANSMITTERS

Researchers are having more success in better understanding how addiction can hijack the brain by turning its reward circuits against itself.

The neurotransmitter dopamine, for example, has received a lot of scientific attention. Dopamine is a key chemical messenger in the brain that helps with a wide array of functions, from simple movement to feelings of enjoyment. The best-known dopamine-related pathology may be Parkinson's disease, caused by the death of those brain cells that normally secrete the chemical. Without dopamine, the brain doesn't send signals to the muscles so that they can function properly.

But dopamine also causes the euphoria that accompanies emotions and pleasure, including those that arise from everything from good food to exercise to sex. (Fact is, it's not simple infatuation that makes us joyful, giddy, and obsessive when in the first flush of love but rather some very potent brain chemistry.)

The problem for some people is that alcohol interferes with the brain's neurotransmitters, tricking the brain into producing dopamine and giving them the same sense of elation from being intoxicated as when they fall in love or eat a five-star dinner. Worse, over time, alcohol takes over their reward system, dominating the production of dopamine to the exclusion of the healthy activities that used to kick its production into gear. Worst of all is that the effects of alcohol taper off over time, forcing people to drink more and more in order to enjoy the same happy feelings.

Researchers aren't certain why some people are susceptible to this kind of self-sabotage while others aren't. One theory is that individuals who are predisposed to becoming alcoholics are born with lower dopamine levels. Why they have lower dopamine levels is uncertain, but they experience fewer natural highs than others do, and they are forever trying to make up the difference.

Despite lingering questions, drug companies are barreling ahead with developing drugs that aim to hamper dopamine's pleasurable signals and free addicts from its control. Among those parts of the brain in their sights is a group of dopamine receptors called D3 that seem to proliferate when certain individuals use certain drugs. Research has already shown that blocking these D3 receptors can dampen much of alcohol's effects.

BIG PHARMA'S SOLUTIONS

Big pharmaceutical companies are also working on ways to enhance the brain's natural damping circuit, called GABA (gamma-aminobutyric acid), in the hope of arming addicts with a way to control their cravings.

Prometa, for example, a drug owned by a publicly traded company in Los Angeles called Hythiam, claims to help addicts— specifically people addicted to methamphetamines or cocaine— maintain their abstinence by reducing their cravings and reversing the damaging adaptations that have occurred in their brains.

Whether it works remains to be seen. Hythiam issued a press release that showed the results of the first study comparing Prometa to a placebo in November 2007. In the 30-day study, 67 methamphetamine-addicted subjects were given Prometa and 67 received a placebo. Although methamphetamine cravings dropped in both groups, it dropped 31.1 points in the group that took Prometa compared to 20.9 points in the placebo group, a statistically significant difference. But the study was funded by Hythiam, the company that owns the drug. (Hythiam insists that it had no control over the data or its analysis.)

Several other pharmaceutical companies are studying the effects of another drug, vigabatrin, on the brains of cocaine and methamphetamine users. Vigabatrin was developed as a treatment for epilepsy. Researchers are hoping that vigabatrin, an effective GABA booster, will help addicts keep their cravings in check.

OTHER AREAS OF RESEARCH:
SEROTONIN AND P300S

Scientists are also learning more about the connection between the addict's brain and his or her serotonin levels. Some believe that serotonin, a chemical produced as a response to a food or an activity—it tells the brain to stop eating when its owner is full, for example—doesn't tell alcoholics to stop drinking as it does with nonalcoholics.

Again, although research has shown that alcoholics seem to have poorly working serotonin systems, no one has been able to determine why conclusively. In one recent example, researchers used the antidepressant drug citalopram, commonly known as Celexa, to bind to the serotonin "transporter," the site in the serotonin system responsible for turning off serotonin production. The team then examined 12 healthy but alcohol-dependent men and 14 healthy nonalcoholic men, observing the responses of three hormones known to multiply when the serotonin system is excited.[2] The citalopram, administered in two separate sessions to both groups of men, did virtually nothing.

Scientists are far from giving up, though. Among other avenues that they are exploring are brain waves related to impulsiveness—P-300s—because these brain waves appear to be smaller and slower in the brains of alcoholics. What researchers hope to determine in the not-too-distant future is whether prolonged exposure to alcohol short-circuits the brain waves, or whether individuals are born with smaller, slower P-300s, predisposing them to alcoholism. (Young children of alcoholics can have the same issue, research has found.[3])

Can Science Fix Addiction?

In short, there is good news—progress is being made in the treatment of addiction—and there is bad news—science is still working on its physical origins.

In time, more answers about the physical components of addiction will come. For example, the neurochemistry of depression is much better known than that of happiness, mostly because depression has been studied more intensively and for much longer. Similarly, researchers have, relatively speaking, only begun to examine why we become addicted.

Still, since addiction disrupts so many brain regions, it's extremely unlikely that researchers will ever be able to pinpoint a single neurological "cause." And while studies are now being conducted into the effects of other addiction-related genes and brain circuits, it's unlikely that anyone will develop an antiaddiction medication any time soon.

In some ways, that may be a blessing. Even if a drug turns out to have the promised effect, it will be nothing more than a stop-gap measure. It might prevent addicts from getting high, but it wouldn't stop them from looking for a quick fix every time they feel bad. In time, it's likely that their addiction would reinvent itself, attaching itself to a new drug or perhaps to an addictive behavior, such as gambling or eating.

Researchers may not ever be able to pinpoint a single neurological "cause" for addiction because it disrupts the normal functions of more than one region in the brain.

In fact, dishing out an antiaddiction pill could actually worsen an addict's condition by perpetuating the quick-fix mind-set. (AA members use the phrase "dry drunk" to describe someone who has quit drinking without fundamentally changing his or her behavior.)

Change, improvement, well-being *is* possible. But in order to beat addiction, people need much more than an antiaddiction pill.

Addicts need to tackle the underlying emotional and psychiatric issues. And while trying to find the reason why some who try drugs get hooked and why some who drink become alcoholics is a highly valuable pursuit, it doesn't change one key point: Addiction doesn't happen in a vacuum. The difference between those who are simply susceptible to addiction and those who become addicts is ultimately who has the healthier emotional life.

Recognizing Emotions

If emotional trauma is responsible for addiction, you might ask yourself what makes up our emotions? Whether we are talking about subjective feelings generated by thoughts or unconscious responses to stimuli, emotions are a prime determinant of the sense of individual well-being.

As a psychoanalyst, I have found a spectrum of everyday feelings that are closely linked to addiction, including shame, humiliation, anger, and despair. They are so present in the everyday actions of addicts that they have become second nature. A critical challenge with addicts is to identify these feelings and understand that they can be managed. One of the most common characteristics of depression is that people assume the worst about themselves, which makes self-destructive behavior possible. To discover the healthy mental state inside, a person first has to recognize the emotions that he or she is currently experiencing as negative. After that, it is a slow but nevertheless reachable path to let them go.

Everyday feelings, such as shame, humiliation, anger, and despair can be linked to addiction.

PART II

Recovery

❦

The Challenges of Treatment

HOW TO STOP

WHEN YOU RECOGNIZE THAT addiction is a two-pronged problem, you can see why it's so hard to treat.

An unresolved emotional trauma can lead to a psychological problem such as anxiety, paranoia, or depression. Ninety-nine percent of addicts in my care suffer from one or more of these disorders.

If we don't take the time to understand an emotional condition, a treatment program could actually intensify an unnoticed disorder. When therapy deals with childhood trauma, it can bring up strong negative emotions that put the patient at risk of relapse. Alcohol and sedative withdrawal will aggravate any preexisting problems such as anxiety or even panic disorders. People use addictions as an escape from emotional issues yet, ironically, drug and alcohol can worsen such issues. The addict is then driven back to the object of his addiction, a vicious cycle develops, and drug and alcohol use spiral out of control.

Once caught in such a cycle it is very difficult for people with a physiological dependence on narcotics and alcohol to stop using. The numbers support this. About 70 percent of patients in treatment relapse in the first year.[1] Addiction is a stubborn disease.

One person caught in such a cycle and successfully treated at Creative Care two years ago was a retired police chief from central California. For years, this patient, Charlie, had struggled with upsetting memories from his days on the job. He rarely slept. When his wife died unexpectedly, her passing pushed him over the edge. He began to drink more and more heavily. With prodding from friends and former colleagues, he tried several times to stop on his own. He went to local Alcoholics Anonymous meetings. He tried practicing the 12 Steps. But he couldn't quit, and once he was on his own in the home he had shared with his wife, the situation rapidly deteriorated to the point that Charlie's son feared that his father might die. The son intervened, bringing him to us.

It was no surprise that Charlie wasn't able to help himself. As we determined by observing him and listening to his self-reported experiences, Charlie was suffering from posttraumatic stress disorder (PTSD), a disorder that first began to impact him while he was still with the police department.

SUBSTANCE ABUSE AND SEVERE
EMOTIONAL ISSUES

What did Charlie's condition have to do with his excessive drinking? And how do we know that his PTSD was exacerbating his addiction to alcohol and vice versa?

To understand how trauma can lead to emotional distress and affect alcohol consumption, it's important to understand the biochemical changes that occur during and after a traumatic experience.

During trauma, the body secretes endorphins to help numb the pain.[2] But afterward, when those endorphins taper off, that endorphin withdrawal can cause the symptoms of emotional distress observed after a traumatic event. Drinking allows people to mask those endorphin withdrawal symptoms—at least, for a while. But chronic exposure to this cycle often leads to alcoholism.

You see, PTSD typically occurs in people who have been exposed to a potentially life-threatening situation during which they experience an acute sense of fear or horror.

Other extremely traumatic events, such as witnessing someone die or be seriously injured, also can prompt symptoms of PTSD, which can include nightmares and flashbacks along with active avoidance of any reminder of the event. (Sufferers tend to steer clear of places or people who remind them of their painful trauma; it's the body's way of trying to detach itself from the pain.)

It's important to note that experiencing trauma doesn't necessarily lead to PTSD or, for that matter, to any psychiatric disorder. If everyone who experienced a traumatic event developed PTSD, many, many more people would be diagnosed with it than is the case today. According to the National Institutes of Health (NIH), roughly 70 percent of Americans have gone through at least one trauma, ranging from sexual abuse to a traffic accident.[3] Most manage to get past those experiences and go on to lead healthy emotional lives. Unfortunately, about 8 percent do not. Worse, the consequences of the trauma that they have experienced worsen over time.

Such was the case with Charlie, whose painful memories of a shooting while he was on active duty grew more painful over time.

BIOCHEMISTRY OF ADDICTION

Let's go back to those biochemical changes that occur during and after a traumatic experience and that can create a heightened desire to drink. Our experience and NIH research reveal a strong correlation between PTSD and alcoholism.

In NIH research involving rats,[4] electric shocks elevated the rats' stress hormone levels. Immediately afterward, the same rats demonstrated an increased alcohol preference. How? Each group of rats learned that by pressing a bar, they could access as much alcohol as they wanted to drink. One group of rats received random shocks; the other group received shocks that they were able to control. The traumatized rats gulped down substantially more alcohol.

Perhaps most interestingly, the increases in alcohol consumption were modest in the immediate aftermath of the shocks, but subsequently, the rats demonstrated a preference for dramatically more alcohol. The reason? Unlike the rats that could control when they would be shocked, the rats whose shocks were beyond their control learned that their responses to such trauma were of *no consequence.* Helpless, they increased their alcohol intake.

The NIH researchers also identified a strong association between alcoholism and PTSD by looking at a sample of Vietnam veterans, roughly half of whom showed signs of alcoholism.[5]

They, too, drank more following—but not during—exposure to stress.

The reason that people turn to alcohol *after* a stressful event, rather than to alleviate anxiety while it's happening, lies in the biology of the stress response.

You see, fear compels a chain of events, beginning with the release of a hormone called adrenocorticotropic hormone (ACTH) and ending in the release of a neurotransmitter called beta-endorphin. The beta-endorphin acts as an analgesic; it numbs both physical and emotional pain. It's why we start to feel better immediately after an acute physical trauma, even though the symptoms are still present.

Trauma causes the release of both ACTH and beta-endorphins, but repeated trauma causes people's pain response to decrease. The reason is that chronic stimulation of the stress response causes the ACTH to overpower the beta-endorphins. This means that people suffering from PTSD—people who essentially suffer from their trauma time and time again—are experiencing more and more pain, something for which drinking alcohol (which can increase endorphin activity) compensates.

WHAT CAN CAUSE TRAUMA?

Back to Charlie, whose problems began when he was involved in a 911 call that went awry, resulting in his failure to stop a double homicide.

Police departments often have stress management teams that make every effort to help officers, and Charlie did work with someone directly after the shooting. But invariably, life went on. His case manager moved on to other crises, and Charlie, who underestimated the incident's impact on him, was left alone with his thoughts.

Though he was aware that minor events were causing him unease in a way that they never had—a car backfiring, a surprise tap on the shoulder—his escalating anxiety wasn't apparent to him at first.

Soon, however, his anxiety had begun to consume him. First he began to have frequent nightmares. Later he became more sensitive to the creaks and groans of his own home, sure that there was an assailant in one of its rooms. His wife tried to help him, but it was impossible to snap him out of his state. In fact, not only did he remember every detail of the scene that haunted him, but he began to replay it in his mind more and more often and to drink greater amounts as the memory became harder to deal with, which made the scenes even more ghastly.

Several years later, widowed and more alone with his thoughts than ever, Charlie was on the brink of alcohol poisoning.

It's a shame that he suffered for as long as he did, because once he was diagnosed with PTSD, we were able to alleviate a lot of pain he'd been carrying around—since even before that 911 call.

If someone with PTSD has developed a drug and alcohol issue, you need to assess whether another trauma took place earlier in his or her life. Often issues that come up later in life retrigger an initial trauma. Even those rare people who can make the connection between the two traumas by themselves don't have the tools to analyze the problem completely.

My supposition is always that if you have a trauma-free life growing up, and you experience trauma as an adult, you can navigate your way through it. You may get bogged down for a while, but you won't get stuck.

Individuals who have suffered from early unresolved trauma are usually knocked out when a fresh trauma occurs.

With Charlie, the first step was getting him through detox. Next, we evaluated him, as we do all our patients, to see if he might have bipolar disorder or other physiological conditions. When we realized that he was suffering from PTSD, we began to work on the trauma issue. It wasn't easy, of course. But at Creative Care, we talk through the trauma event and really try to bring to light what the patient is out of touch with. Often we discover that someone was molested or otherwise abused by a parent or caregiver. In Charlie's case, we learned that his own mother was a neglectful alcoholic who left him home alone for days at a time when he was a young child. Painful as it was, we helped him review that experience, take inventory, and start to put the pieces together. Once he made the connection, he no longer needed to anesthetize himself. He knew where the pain was, and that knowledge helped him overcome it.

QUESTIONS OF CAUSE AND CONSEQUENCE CONUNDRUM

Tackling addiction is sometimes challenging because drugs and emotional or psychiatric problems display many of the same symptoms, and it can be hard to tell whether a symptom is the result of drug use or an underlying condition. For example, alcoholism can cause dissociation, or periods of lost time, but so can PTSD. Drug use can mask as well as mimic psychiatric symptoms. And someone with bipolar disorder might use alcohol to slow down during manic periods.

To further confuse matters, psychiatric symptoms may be a sign of a physical illness. For instance, I once treated a patient who had become psychotic as a result of end-stage liver failure.

Indeed, many times psychiatric symptoms overwhelm their physical manifestations. What might seem like a clear-cut case of anxiety neuroses actually can be caused by an overactive thyroid gland or too little glucose in the blood (hypoglycemia). What appears to be schizophrenia or paranoia can be caused by inflamed blood vessels owing to collagen disease, or a pancreatic tumor, or a number of other things. Even violent behavior sometimes is caused by medical illness or has some other physical etiology. A physical exam is necessary to rule out physical illness as a cause or contributing factor to addiction.

Often the biggest challenge to treating addicts is engaging them as active participants in their recovery from both addiction and emotional issues.

I'd like to tell you about two patients who came to Creative Care in the late 1990s: Elizabeth, who was one of our biggest uphill battles, but we were able to treat her successfully; Jonah, however, we still consider one of our biggest missed opportunities.

ELIZABETH'S STORY

Elizabeth lived in Los Angeles with her second husband, a former television executive 16 years her senior who also had been married once before. Both had been married to their first loves. Elizabeth was wed for seven years to her high school boyfriend; her husband spent a dozen years married to his college girlfriend.

Elizabeth and her second husband had met decades earlier at the television station where they both worked—he as a manager, she as a reporter. Together they had three children—two sons and one daughter.

Mostly, however, they were different people from different backgrounds. He was the son of schoolteachers and enjoyed a middle-class upbringing, Elizabeth's wealthy, well-educated family had owned and sold a prominent national chain of retail stores.

Elizabeth's husband had spent his career as do many people of his means: with a respectable but modest safety net. Elizabeth had, and always would, receive money from a trust fund. In fact, when his career became permanently derailed after he lost a key promotion, Elizabeth's money supported the couple and their children.

You might think: aha! Elizabeth greatly resented being responsible for the family's financial well-being. And she did. But Elizabeth's resentment was more deeply seated than she realized.

At Creative Care, she complained of one missed opportunity after another: she turned down education at Columbia University so that she could be closer to the man who would become her first husband. That first marriage, in which she invested so much of herself, ended in heartbreak and divorce.

Indeed, by the time she was reluctantly dragged to our doorstep, Elizabeth was drinking two bottles of wine a day, her sons had stopped talking to her, and her husband, who had convinced her to enter an addiction clinic months earlier (she'd gone but relapsed soon after leaving), was contemplating divorce. After more than 20 years of marriage, in which Elizabeth acted belligerently toward him on an increasingly regular basis, he'd had enough.

He also admitted that he had little sympathy for the abandonment issues with which she was struggling, including anticipatory anxiety as they prepared their youngest child for college. In fact, he and the children told me that they felt emotionally drained by Elizabeth, who never hesitated to complain about the great things that she imagined for herself yet didn't have, from a more successful husband, to a longer career for herself in television, to a happier childhood.

Still, even with her family life falling apart around her, Elizabeth hadn't hit bottom when she came to Creative Care. She wasn't convinced that she had permanently damaged her relationship with her children, and she didn't believe that her husband—now dependent on her financially—would move forward with divorce proceedings.

The good news for the entire family was that even though Elizabeth had not yet bought into the 12 Steps, her coming to Creative Care signaled that she recognized that her drinking was out of control.

Further—and equally as important—based on Elizabeth's self-reported experiences to our psychotherapists and the information provided us by her husband and children, we were able to diagnose her with bipolar disorder, a brain disorder that causes unusual shifts in a person's mood, energy, and ability to function. This disorder sometimes can be identified initially by the sufferer's highly negative, chaotic interpersonal relationships.

ACCEPTING A DIAGNOSIS

The diagnosis would prove the key to Elizabeth's recovery. But first, she had to accept that she had a serious issue whose cause still baffles many experts in the health industry. Scientists believe that genes play a big role, as bipolar disorder tends to run in families. Unfortunately, they have yet to identify the specific genes at its root. They only know that, like other psychiatric conditions, bipolar disorder isn't caused by a single gene.[6]

It's not surprising that Elizabeth had lived her life plagued by bipolar disorder but unaware of it. About 5.7 million American adults, or just less than 3 percent of the population age 18 and older in any given year, have bipolar disorder.[7] It usually develops in a person's late teens or in early adulthood, though some people experience their first symptoms as children and others experience them later in life.

Unfortunately, bipolar disorder often goes unrecognized as an illness. People just like Elizabeth sometimes suffer for years before it is properly diagnosed and treated.

What we do know about bipolar disorder is that likely it is caused by many different genes acting together, and in combination with other factors, including an individual's environment.

Finding the offending genes is an ongoing endeavor for scientists. Brain-imaging studies are helping them determine where things go wrong in the brain to produce the condition. Already evidence from imaging studies strongly suggests that the brains of individuals with bipolar disorder differ from the brains of those who are healthy.[8]

Even as we await more research and improved science, there are many ways to identify bipolar disorder. Nearly all of the identifying features hounded Elizabeth, and made her diagnosis relatively simple.

The biggest distinguishing feature of bipolar disorder is dramatic mood swings—highs and lows known as episodes of mania and depression. Signs of a manic period include extreme irritability; spending sprees; increased sexual drive; provocative, aggressive, or intrusive behavior; denial that anything is wrong; racing thoughts and talking quickly; and drug abuse, including cocaine, alcohol, and sleeping medications.

Signs of a depressive episode include lingering feelings of sadness; feelings of hopelessness and/or worthlessness; loss of interest in sex; fatigue; either oversleeping or an inability to sleep; and suicidal thoughts or outright attempts at suicide.

Manic episodes tend to last at least one week; depressive episodes last two weeks or more.

One of the biggest challenges to treatment success is engaging people as active participants in their own recovery.

Elizabeth had lived this emotional roller coaster for decades. For some time after coming to Creative Care, Elizabeth denied that anything was wrong with her outside of her addiction to alcohol.

Among other arguments against why she did not "have a mental illness," she explained that she enjoyed long periods free of any symptoms of bipolar disorder. It wasn't difficult to believe. In between episodes of mania and depression—which can be chronic to recurrent but infrequent throughout one's life—individuals with bipolar disorder truly are free of symptoms.

But Elizabeth's resistance made our work all the more challenging, because even *when* a patient accepts the diagnosis of bipolar disorder, it's a very difficult condition to treat.

WHETHER TO MEDICATE

Let's take a break here to address those emotional issues—including bipolar disorder—whose treatment combines both psychosocial treatment and medication.

With bipolar disorder, medications called mood stabilizers typically are prescribed because the condition is recurrent and lifelong and usually requires long-term treatment—meaning years.

Most people being treated for bipolar disorder are given lithium, which has been around seemingly forever (it was the first mood-stabilizing drug approved by the U.S. Food and Drug

Administration for children ages 12 and older). It is still the most effective mood-stabilizing medication for controlling mania and preventing the recurrence of both depressive and manic episodes.

But sometimes additional meds are prescribed for shorter periods, as when an episode of mania or depression overwhelms the mood stabilizer. For example, meds known as valproates or carbamazepines can be particularly useful for hard-to-treat bipolar episodes. Valproates are chemical compounds that are also used as anticonvulsants and treat a wide variety of conditions, including epilepsy, migraine headaches, and schizophrenia, as well as bipolar disorder. Similarly, carbamazepines are anticonvulsants used to treat not only bipolar disorder but epilepsy, schizophrenia, attention deficit disorder, and attention deficit hyperactivity disorder.

The drugs do have a downside. Like nearly every medication, they have side effects, including weight gain, nausea, decreased sexual drive, anxiety, hair loss, tremors, or dry mouth—though a change in the prescribed dosage can relieve all of these problems.

The medications are necessary because they protect individuals with bipolar disorder from rapid cycling between high and low episodes, which can cause anguish to afflicted individuals and the people who love them.

Let me be clear: I don't advocate treating addiction with medication. But I do strongly believe in the inarguable benefits of many nonnarcotic, nonaddictive medications, particularly many that have emerged in the last 5 to 15 years.

Thankfully, after some time, Elizabeth agreed to try medication, and it made her far more willing to undergo the second part of her treatment: psychotherapy, which leads to far better functioning. I've seen it time and again in my own practice, and studies support as much.[9] In psychotherapy, our staff taught Elizabeth how to better regulate her emotions, new coping skills, and other cognitive restructuring.

We knew what to do because we see a lot of Elizabeths. Alcohol and drug abuse are very common among people with bipolar disorder because they try to self-medicate their severe moodiness.

Elizabeth deserves most of the credit for her recovery, however. By accepting that she was more than simply an alcoholic—by recognizing that she had serious emotional issues that needed to be addressed if she was ever to overcome her reliance on alcohol—she has been able to move forward in her life.

Elizabeth and her husband went on to divorce, but by learning to manage her disorder effectively and without alcohol, today she is happily remarried and has a better relationship with her three children.

JONAH'S STORY

Presumably you are beginning to see that, while difficult, an accurate diagnosis is essential because once addicts get into treatment, an undiagnosed condition could undermine their recovery. Emotional issues may prevent people from staying sober. Conversely, if people continue to use drugs and alcohol, this behavior will jeopardize their psychiatric treatment.

Sometimes the failure to address both issues can be fatal. Such was the case with Jonah, another former patient of Creative Care. Even now, years later, it still pains me that we were unable to help him.

A 19-year-old heroin addict from the Midwest, Jonah came to us after spending 28 days at another facility, where he had undergone detox. No doubt the process had been excruciating.

A heroin addict's nervous system becomes accustomed to chronic use of the drug, which is a natural opioid—a chemical substance with morphinelike, pain-relieving effects on the body. Withdrawal from heroin causes extreme abdominal pain, insomnia, chills, sweating, and diarrhea, just to name a few symptoms. Even in a medically supervised setting, using anesthetics such as the synthetic, nonnarcotic opioid methadone (which can make withdrawal far less painful), the process can lead to delirium, psychosis, and acute renal failure, if not death.

Little wonder that the average heroin addict will try to detox and fail numerous times in his or her lifetime. Indeed, in a 2001 University of California, Los Angeles, study, researchers conducted a 33-year follow-up of nearly 600 heroin addicts and concluded that though five years of abstaining from the drug considerably increased the likelihood that they would not relapse, roughly one-quarter of the addicts still experienced relapse even after 15 years of abstinence.[10]

Jonah had made it through several weeks of detoxification and counseling at the other facility, but his counselors realized that he suffered from depression and that to ensure his recovery, he would need more than they could offer. (As you know by this point, addiction treatment programs typically focus on their patients' addictions, viewing psychiatric symptoms as secondary. In most instances, only when a patient has a severe psychiatric disorder, such as schizophrenia, does he or she enter a psychiatric facility, where his or her addiction takes a backseat to the psychiatric care administered there.)

The facility told Jonah's family about us, and it was our intention to determine whether he had emotional issues that compelled him to use heroin, or if the heroin—which can cause feelings of severe depression—had caused his emotional problems.

But Jonah wasn't committed to his own recovery. After just two days at Creative Care, he told us flatly that he wanted to leave and that his mother (who'd brought him to us as soon as he left the other clinic) was aware that he wanted to leave.

I will always remember Jonah casually saying that his mother was "fine with it."

I wanted to keep him, but he wasn't actively suicidal, so we couldn't physically or legally hold him. All we could do was phone his mother, who said that her son talked with her about leaving and told her that he was feeling better.

She desperately wanted to believe that Jonah was happy and healthy, so she gave him the support he craved; she didn't want him to feel fenced in. Yet not a week after he'd left us, he was discovered dead in another state. He had procured more heroin from someone, and he had overdosed. Because his system had recently been cleared of opiates, the dose he took, his usual, overwhelmed his system.

It was a devastating outcome, and as someone who knows the pain of losing a loved one, I still ache for his family. It was also a defeat for us because Jonah was severely depressed, and we didn't have the opportunity to figure out why and to help him.

HOW WE GET AT THE EMOTIONAL
ROOT OF TRAUMA

Again, treating addiction and emotional issues concurrently is essential to recovery, but it's also highly challenging. As I mentioned, addicts can be difficult to treat because drugs and emotional or psychiatric problems cause many of the same symptoms, and it can be hard to tell whether a symptom is the result of drug use or an underlying condition. More, disorders often exacerbate one another. Although many people who turn to alcohol or drugs use them—often unwittingly—to escape their emotional issues, their substance abuse almost always makes such issues worse, which drives them back to the object of their addiction in an agonizing loop.

Concentrating too much on the addiction piece of the puzzle can also be dangerous. Earlier in the book, I pointed out that alcohol and sedative withdrawal can worsen panic disorder. And that's saying nothing of the fact that psychiatric symptoms may be a sign of a physical illness. A neurological disorder called Huntington's, symptoms of which include anxiety, depression, and sometimes even hypersexuality, is often misdiagnosed as schizophrenia. Head injuries often cause personality changes and sometimes even schizophrenia-like symptoms. The list goes on and on.

Yet one of the most tremendous challenges of all is enlisting someone in the battle for his or her life, as you saw with both Elizabeth and Jonah.

Nevertheless, if treatment for only one of two coexisting conditions is successful, relapse is not only likely but practically assured.

HOW DO WE MEASURE RECOVERY?

Recovery is a gift.

Individuals who have battled addiction will tell you that they are thankful for every day that they are sober. Therapists advise taking things one day at a time, but I will go further and ask that addicts take the long view of life. Will sobriety last a lifetime? Will it last 5 or 10 years? This is a question that no one can answer. Life is messy, and there will be many ups and downs. But in the long view, patients who are committed to recovery travel an upward incline.

~
𝒸

Facing Yourself
through Therapy

*In order to put the past behind you, you must put it in front
of you.*

KNOWING THE TRAUMAS PEOPLE have experienced in their
lives and understanding the impact of those traumas is
crucial to understanding why they become addicts, and
how their addictions can be overcome.

By the time we are adults, we have all enjoyed triumph and
defeat, pride and humiliation, sorrow and bliss. We have also all
experienced challenges, though what kinds and how we dealt
with them vary as dramatically as they inform who we become.
Losing my mother when I was a teenager has much to do with
why I became a psychoanalyst, for example. Years later, losing an
alcoholic brother to suicide put me on a second path, to becoming an addiction expert.

Given my history, I, too, could have succumbed to alcoholism,
but I didn't. Why not? The answer owes partly to serendipity and

luck. As I mentioned earlier, because of graduate school requirements, I had to undergo 50 hours of psychoanalysis over the course of one year. I was 28 at the time. But that year was such a revelation that it became an 18-year journey for me, one that started when my psychoanalyst asked me to put my past in front of me and to examine it.

Confronting the past wasn't comfortable. I didn't necessarily believe that my past needed to be unearthed and examined. My psychoanalyst was determined, though. Not only did he have me rifle through my past, but he had me relive, rethink, and reframe it. As trite as it might sound now, those exercises probably saved my life. I had no idea how much baggage I was carrying around until I was able to shake loose some of it and to organize and prioritize what I needed to keep.

Since that time, I've done my best to instill in each of my patients, including those at Creative Care, the realization that you have to face yourself. It's why we set up our program as we do. Most addiction treatment facilities, as I've mentioned, keep their patients busy with meetings from daybreak to evening to keep them distracted from their physical cravings (and the opportunity to indulge them). We take a very different approach. Although we, too, schedule our fair share of meetings, they are all almost all aimed at examining the addicts' interior lives. More, as noted earlier, we schedule plenty of "alone" time, during which we ask our patients to be introspective and to reacquaint themselves with the person whom they've been suppressing with alcohol and/or drugs.

The reason we do this is because addicts are self-loathing. Even in the deepest throes of addiction, they are aware that they are killing themselves. Most addicts essentially make a pact with themselves that they can accept death as the most likely outcome of their actions. This is the reason why, once addicts have stopped abusing drugs or alcohol, they need to relearn to love themselves quickly; if they can't, they risk slipping back into the darkness.

Self-love comes from within, of course. It comes from sitting with yourself and relearning how to be in your own skin. And even though addicts typically don't like free time, at least not initially, eventually most realize that it's an instrumental step in the ongoing path toward recovery.

Addiction is a chronic, recurring illness that requires lifelong attention.

Many recovering addicts commit themselves to 12 Step programs such as Alcoholics Anonymous and Narcotics Anonymous, both of which provide simple tools for living based on spiritual principles and—possibly more important—the fellowship of other people who share their experience with addiction and who support one another.

At Creative Care, we have pioneered a treatment method known as "psychodynamic therapy." It is more direct and focused than standard psychotherapy. Its premise is that a more a intensive and brief intervention can achieve more effective results than the more tradicional psychoanalytic practice of allowing the client to freely discuss unconnected issues. Singling out the most important issue creates a structure and identifies a goal for the treatment. In psychodynamic therapy we strive to help the client understand the unconscious processes that manifest themselves destructively in their behavior. We help them examine the unresolved conflicts and symptoms that manifest themselves as substance abuse.

The change and healing process typically require one to two years. This is because the goal of therapy is to change an aspect of one's identity. It relies on the interpersonal relationship between client and therapist and involves a lot of community interaction.

We ask all of our patients to join in 12 Step meetings, which we hold on-site in the evenings, and we strongly encourage them to join meetings in their own communities when they return home or start new lives elsewhere. The organizations have proven to be godsends to addicts, who struggle against their demons every single day. Little wonder that there are so many membership groups. Roughly 54,000 Alcoholics Anonymous groups have formed in the United States since the program was first developed by a small group of alcoholics 65 years ago, and they've drawn more than 1.2 million members.[1]

Yet because addiction always has strong emotional underpinnings, I also believe very strongly in the role of psychotherapy, or "talk therapy," in recovery, particularly at the outset of the process. As I keep saying, without identifying an addict's core emotional issues and addressing them, recovery is unsustainable.

Two schools of psychotherapy that we use at Creative Care are psychodynamic and cognitive therapy.

"Psychotherapy" is a general term for talk therapy. On a practical level, cognitive therapy is rooted in the belief that learned processes play a crucial role in the development of maladaptive behavioral patterns and that individuals can learn to identify those behaviors and stop them. Cognitive therapy often lasts just a short time: about 12 weeks; and participants often are assigned "homework" to complete between sessions.

Behavioral therapy is the form of cognitive therapy that has gained the most ground in recent decades. In my opinion, it is the most helpful therapy for people overcoming addiction. It focuses on modifying overt behavior and helping people to set and achieve concrete goals. (It's often called cognitive behavioral therapy.)

Of course, cognitive therapy is effective only when people are ready for it and willing to cooperate. But assuming that someone is working with a good therapist, one who knows how to function as a coach and teacher and who can foster a positive, encouraging relationship, cognitive therapy can work wonders.

Studies show that cognitive therapy can reduce the rate of repeated suicide attempts by 50 percent during a year of follow-up.

A previous suicide attempt is about the strongest predictor of suicide, and cognitive therapy helps those who attempt it to consider alternatives when thoughts of harming themselves arise.[2]

There's also evidence that the benefits of cognitive therapy last longer than the benefits of medication for people with certain emotional issues, including panic disorder, posttraumatic stress disorder, and social phobia.

And studies have shown that certain forms of cognitive therapy are very helpful to people with bipolar disorder and that psychosocial interventions can lead to increased mood stability and fewer hospitalizations.[3]

Next we turn to a discussion of some of the cognitive therapies that are available today, and that I know from my own experience to work.

COMMUNITY REINFORCEMENT APPROACH

The cognitive behavioral approach known as the community reinforcement approach (CRA) aims to make abstinence more rewarding than addiction. Making sobriety more appealing to an addict is a tall order, of course, but CRA is effective. It works by focusing on the same environmental factors that tip the scales in the direction of addiction in the first place. You see, while family, friends, work, and recreational influences can conspire to turn someone who is already at risk into an addict, those same influences can play a role in helping an addict recover. For instance, the addict might be taught a new vocational skill, or a better way of communicating, or new places to socialize, replacing old activities associated with his or her drinking or drug abuse.

Consider this: As people become increasingly alcohol dependent, the range of what they do shrinks considerably. Forget hobbies, sports, or social involvements. As a consequence, an important factor in addicts' recovery is to get them involved again in their community, including through activities that they can enjoy with nondrinkers. Their clean-living new friends can be recovering alcoholics, by the way, and they often are. Racing for Recovery, a seven-year-old, Ohio-based foundation, encourages people battling with dependency to exercise as a way to add much-needed structure in their lives. More than 2,000 people have run races in various cities around the country thanks to the foundation, and the conditioning helps its participants both to stay sober and to establish and meet goals that they set for themselves.

In fact, a big component of CRA is social and recreational counseling to help recovering addicts find or relearn various activities that they enjoy. Toward this end, the therapist and individual might do what's called activity sampling of activities between counseling sessions, planning where the individual will go and when, how, and who will participate with the recovering addict in those activities.

MOTIVATIONAL ENHANCEMENT TRAINING

Motivational enhancement training (MET) is another approach that zeroes in on addicts' seeming ambivalence about their issues and turns it on its head. How? By showing addicts that they are capable of changing their problematic behaviors.

A key factor in the success of MET centers on the clinician working with the individual. It's important that the clinician does not champion the benefits that abstinence can confer but rather champion the patient's *ability to make decisions for him- or herself*, decisions that are going to positively impact the person's life.

That's not a small nuance. Although counselors may offer advice, including reasons to quit or change, and although they may highlight discrepancies between the individual's behavior and goals, counselors don't say "You must do X, Y, and Z." With MET, addiction issues are viewed as partially voluntary and subject to the normal principles of behavior change. So emphasis is put on eliciting a commitment to change rather than coercing it.

Self-motivation is necessary. Without it, no recovery can last.

MET could not be further from counseling approaches designed to break down an individual's defenses through direct confrontation—an approach that sometimes is necessary and that we at Creative Care occasionally employ. But MET can be exceedingly effective, especially as a prelude to other treatment approaches, because it increases an individual's compliance. (By being the agent of change, the addict becomes a more active participant in his or her own recovery.)

RELAPSE PREVENTION THERAPY

There is a 70 percent chance that a patient will relapse within a year of leaving treatment. Relapse refers to a breakdown or failure in a person's attempt to maintain change in any set of behaviors. It is nearly impossible to get the pace of things perfectly correct the first time around. Sometimes as a recovering addict you might get "homesick" for your life before you embarked on the difficult road to recovery. I teach my patients and their families and friends that this is not a huge setback. Relapse is part of healing. But there are things you can do to scale it back.

This is where Relapse Prevention Therapy comes in. RPT combines behavioral and cognitive interventions in an overall approach that emphasizes self-management. The program teaches you three strategies: The first is coping skills, which teaches clients to identify high-risk situations when you feel like you are craving using. RPT teaches you to control the damage once you do lapse and then it gently teaches you to come back to treatment. Cognitive therapy teaches clients ways to experience the setbacks less as disappointments and more as part of the recovery process. Finally, lifestyle modification strategies such as meditation, exercise, and spiritual practices are designed to strengthen a client's overall coping capacity.

The truth is that often relapse takes you by surprise. In most of the relapse episodes I have studied or worked with clinically, patients report that the first lapse was a complete surprise and took them off guard. They were sailing smoothly toward recovery when they found themselves either with an old drug or drinking buddy or an emotionally painful situation that they used to assuage by using.

It seems that clients unknowingly set themselves up for relapse because they did not or could not see the early warning signs. They might be in denial that they are using or they may be rationalizing their lapse. Here are some warning signs to look for:

- *If you find yourselves or see your recovering loved one withdraw from sober activities. These include going to 12 step meetings, cutting contact with their sponsors, and frequenting people or places where they used to use.*
- *A person may stop taking their nonaddictive medication, usually out of fear that it might poorly interact with addictive substances.*
- *When you or your loved one withdraws from sober support systems, such as seeing family, therapists, friends, and other loved ones.*

Relapse usually begins before a person picks up a substance. In order to avoid relapse a person needs to immediately follow these steps:

- *Don't isolate yourself—turn to stable channels of support and actively discuss the triggers that are causing relapse.*
- *Talk to others who have relapsed.*
- *Put yourself in a safe place that will help stop the downward spiral of feeling out of control.*

Relapse prevention therapy (RPT) is another strategy, one that anticipates the many relapses that most recovering addicts suffer. RPT teaches them how to respond differently every time, until they come upon a way to cope with a high-risk situation without throwing up their hands and having a drink or popping a pill.

RPT works by identifying which situations are the most loaded with temptation because of the stress they cause, and then managing the elated feelings that addicted individuals associate with their substance of choice. For example, it intellectualizes cravings, so that rather than simply falling victim to them, people can think instead about what they are experiencing physiologically.

Like CRA, RPT also helps individuals lead healthier lives on the whole by teaching them strategies like meditation and exercise, strategies that can strengthen people's ability to cope with whatever life throws at them.

Research has shown that RPT works, too, often during treatment,[4] but especially as active treatment is winding down and addicts are entering a period of maintaining their recovery.[5] Indeed, some research shows that RPT is best suited for people in the later stages of treatment or recovery. In the earlier, action stage, people are exposed to a lot of analysis about what led to their substance abuse. That analysis typically motivates people to abstain early on in treatment. In the maintenance stage, however, addicts are focusing on lifestyle changes and on dealing with changes in family and social relationships.

PSYCHODYNAMIC THERAPY

Since addiction is often an attempt to escape from painful emotions, recovery means unearthing and releasing these emotions. Psychotherapy is the most effective way to do this, but often less verbally expressive patients struggle with psychotherapy. Other addicts may find that their trauma is so painful and deeply buried that verbalizing it requires Herculean effort. More, traumas that are experienced during the preverbal stage—as an infant or very young child—are very difficult to translate into words. (These traumas might include the early loss of a family member or lack of maternal attention due to postpartum depression.) The good news is that a number of innovative, nonverbal therapies can help, including eye movement desensitization and reprocessing (EMDR), equine therapy, therapeutic massage, and meditation.

Eye Movement Desensitization and Reprocessing

When people experience a trauma, it's often sealed off in their subconsciousness, which prevents them from processing it emotionally. In the short term, this sealing off is for their own protection, but in the long term, it can have disastrous consequences, such as unpredictable flashbacks, headaches, and sleeplessness, and addiction.

In EMDR, addicts revisit the trauma, guided through a series of rapid eye movements by a therapist. Patients then process the negative emotions surrounding the trauma. ("Processing" can be as simple as feeling rather than repressing an emotion, since sometimes feeling an emotion can be enough to release it.) The rapid eye movements make accessing these emotions easier.

Equine Therapy

Equine therapy is another valuable treatment, one that dates back more than 30 years. We've found it to be a highly effective tool for trauma resolution and for helping newly sober individuals develop some of the life skills they need in order to stay sober.

Put simply, horses mirror humans in many ways, including emotionally, allowing patients to better understand what they are feeling. For example, horses are very effective when it comes to communicating their level of connection: They may walk away from an individual, become distracted by other horses, or wander up to a patient and vie for his or her attention, at times by nuzzling their heads into the person's chest. (For those who haven't spent much time with horses, it's amazing to discover how compassionate and loving they can be. They're also honest; when a horse communicates something, there's no guesswork involved.)

Horses are also very social creatures, with societal rules and a hierarchy that are very similar to the communities that people form. Indeed, by spending time with horses and coming to understand their pecking order, individuals can better comprehend their own roles, so to speak—specifically, whether they are leaders or followers—and begin exploring the advantages and disadvantages of both.

Interestingly, the horse often chooses the patient, who then builds a relationship with the horse under the guidance of a trained therapist who observes and encourages the patient to groom, lead, and otherwise interact with the horse. Almost as often, though, the patient chooses the horse, and that's nice, too. In fact, in choosing a horse, a person often gets a better sense of him- or herself and how he or she relates to others, because horses have very sharply defined personalities. Usually unwittingly, people will gravitate toward the horse that is most like themselves. Interacting with the horse and observing how it relates to the other horses can offer startling insights on a variety of levels, such as how a person is perceived by others.

There are sundry reasons why the therapy is effective at quickly breaking down barriers, including the horse's tremendous physicality. Horses typically weigh between 1,000 and 1,500 pounds and stand more than seven feet tall. Their size can easily elicit in people feelings of anxiety, fear for personal safety, and a mindfulness of boundaries that can serve as a catalyst for their greater self-awareness.

Another benefit of equine therapy is its setting—in the great outdoors, with all of its elements, which naturally fosters an atmosphere of openness and creates a stage for the unexpected. It's a wonderful way for people to experience emotions as they arise and to sit with them, particularly after they have tried for so long to obliterate those emotions through drugs or alcohol.

Therapeutic Massage

Therapeutic massage is another specific course of therapy we use because of its ability to release buried emotions. It's common for people to feel intense emotion during a massage—even to sometimes cry—because negative, repressed emotions often get stored in the body in the form of back pains, tight hips, or other physical problems. Believe it or not, releasing the tightness in these areas can release those repressed feelings.

We incorporate massage into our integrated care program at Creative Care. It is good for individuals in all stages of quitting drug or alcohol addiction, from withdrawal through detox to abstinence. The reason: Skin is the body's largest sensory organ, and massaging it can alleviate pain, increase alertness, and boost the body's autoimmune response by, among other things, suppressing the body's ability to produce the stress hormone cortisol, a by-product of the adrenal system. (Our nervous system secretes cortisol as part of our fight-or-flight system. Under extreme stress, cortisol can provide a surge of extra energy that enables a person to fight or run, but it also represses the immune system.)

Therapeutic massage is also believed to boost an individual's levels of dopamine, one of the chemical messengers in the brain that helps with a wide array of functions, including feelings of enjoyment.

Perhaps most important, though, the deep relaxation of a massage really enables people to connect with themselves and to feel good. And for recovering addicts who are rediscovering the world, the ability to feel good and anchored, without the benefit of alcohol or other substances, is a pretty wonderful thing.

SUPPLEMENTARY THERAPIES

Other wonderful tools can be used in complementary fashion in addiction treatment. One is education about the disease, along with education around managing it, medicating it, self-monitoring, and recognizing how other conditions may interrelate. The more involved the community in this education, the better: think residential therapy programs, house meetings, group counseling, and other structured group education programs. Naturally, one-on-one programs that educate people with bipolar disorder about the illness and its treatment, as well as how to recognize signs of relapse so that early intervention can be sought before a full-blown illness episode occurs, are also key.

Contingency management is another psychosocial system that uses various rewards to enforce abstinence. For example, people in mental health, addiction treatment, or integrated care settings will be allowed a day pass to Starbucks, say, or even a weekend pass home after they submit a certain number of clean urine samples or after they have completed a task relating to improving their living or work situations. It can sound demoralizing on its face, but in the throes of fighting addiction while trying to get to its emotional roots, it can really work wonders. Contingency management offers the most benefit for addicts who have demonstrated an inability to keep their eyes on the prize: sobriety, or freedom from substance use addiction. And it's been shown to reduce use among addicts whose prognosis of getting well is especially bad because they are addicted to more than one substance.[6]

ALL PIECES OF A PUZZLE

All these therapies form pieces of the puzzle that is the process of recovery.

Just as the word "recovery" has a broad spectrum of meaning, so does a recovery from addiction.

In one sense, addicts are regaining themselves after a period when the disease was overshadowing them and they were hidden behind it. In another sense, they are healing from a trauma and moving forward to a completely different emotional footing. Addicts are becoming different people. This is our goal. But it is a new place to inhabit, and in the beginning, the ground beneath their feet may feel unsupportive.

10

Relapse as Part of Recovery

ALWAYS REMEMBER AND NEVER forget that relapse is part of the process of recovery. Just as other chronic diseases like diabetes occasionally flare up when people fail to take their recommended treatments, addicts slip. In fact, half the time they slip into heavy, sustained use, and 90 percent have short-lived relapses before getting back on the road to wellness.

It's cold comfort to know that it happens to nearly everyone. There's no denying that a relapse can be heartbreaking for everyone involved, especially when so much hard work has gone into a person's sobriety and happiness. But while relapses are very hard to avoid entirely, it is useful to understand more about them, and why, when so much is at stake, they happen nevertheless.

FACTORS LEADING TO RELAPSE

Many factors heighten the chance that someone will relapse. Addicts relapse emotionally before they reach for their drug of choice, which is why in the course of treatment, we try to identify a person's emotional triggers. One familiar scenario we see is adult children of abuse who throw out their sobriety over a conflict that they themselves have sought out. For example, say that a man, as a child, watched his mother being chased or verbally abused by his father. If that man is looking for a reason to drink or take drugs once again, he might pick a fight with a girlfriend or argue with his boss, reliving the trauma and then finding a way to relieve it.

All addicts have particular triggers, depending on their history. I recently had a patient who had a very hard time maintaining himself on New Year's Eve, because of the flood of information and memories that washed over him. Many patients succumb when driving past a liquor store. From sights, to sounds, to smells, to cravings, triggers are everywhere. It takes time to become desensitized to them, which is why most addicts, when they relapse, do so right away. Fresh out of recovery, they simply can't handle that flood of information. They have to get their bearings.

Often an addict has to make it through every birthday, every anniversary of a breakup, every holiday—every possible trigger— over the course of one year to gain solid footing in sobriety.

CAN RELAPSE BE PREVENTED?

In my experience, preventing relapse isn't possible, but national studies suggest that aftercare, such as Alcoholics Anonymous meetings, play a critical role in an addict's long-term recovery. I'd say that 60 percent of our patients who involve themselves in aftercare support groups or meetings are able to maintain their sobriety over the long haul and that between 30 and 40 percent of our patients who don't dedicate themselves to aftercare succumb to relapses time and again. It all comes back to an addict's commitment to recovery.

The good news is that relapse actually can complete the circle of care. Most people don't become fully committed to their recovery until they realize how precious and fragile it is. In fact, as I just mentioned, we don't consider addicts in safe territory until they have had one relapse under their belts. The reason? Every time addicts relapse, it strengthens their intentions, it gives them the incentive to recommit themselves. They start to know what they need to stay focused on and what not to skip (like AA meetings). Beginning the 12 Steps all over again can be painful, but addicts also learn just how powerless they are, and in surrendering again, they are strengthened.

HOW LONG DO PEOPLE RELAPSE?

Relapse can take a month, a week, two years. Sometimes people have a relapse that drags on for a month before they recommit. Sometimes it takes them a year to stop and recommit. As I said, in most cases, when addicts finally do recommit, their recovery is a lot stronger, because they understand how quickly sobriety, and all of the hard work to attain it, can be lost—poof.

Alexis, whom I met six years ago, is a former patient who is herself a trained psychologist, yet even she relapsed once because she simply wasn't committed to her recovery.

ALEXIS'S STORY

Her degree in psychotherapy aside, Alexis is like many of our patients. By the time she came to us, she had already undergone

one stint at a drug treatment facility, but it wasn't able to derail her from the fast track to self-destruction that she was on by her early 30s. A young mother with four children, she was trapped in a marriage that was falling apart. And despite her intellect, training, and financial resources—Alexis's father had founded a highly successful private equity firm—she was hopelessly stuck and slowly killing herself with drugs, a reaction to the severe depression she was mired in. It took the determined involvement of her sister, who had turned her own life around after receiving treatment for depression and addiction, for Alexis to come to us and get the help that she desperately needed. Her story, in her own words, follows.

I was the first of four girls, so I never had much of a childhood. It certainly wasn't carefree. I was always Mother's little helper, doing what I could to keep my mom happy by helping her to take care of the other kids. I was also her little companion, because my father, who was extremely successful, was always busy traveling and generally had other priorities.

It might sound like a quaint picture, a mother and her flock of girls, but it was far from that. My mother was lonely and rage filled, and I always felt very tense, very nervous around her, afraid I'd exacerbate an already sour mood. So I worked hard to make her happy. I knew that as long as everything went along smoothly on any given day, I'd feel better, and I did. It was a relief.

That could only last so long, though. When I was about 13 years old, I finally said something to her about my anxiety. I didn't blame her for it. I was careful of that. I pretended I wasn't sure why I was experiencing it, hoping that she'd put two and two together. But she immediately concluded that I was stress-ridden because of school, and she right away tried to medicate me. Her response was "I see. Take this." I think she gave me belladonna, an herb for menstrual cramps and motion sickness. It wasn't "How can I help you," or "Let's examine this a little bit."

It still amazes me. My mother was the highest-functioning, most controlled alcoholic I've ever seen. She still is, though she'll never admit it. For decades, she's had the same thing to drink, every night, in the exact same amount. But if one of her kids had a problem, she was like "Why? Where does all of this come from?"

I remember in high school one night addressing the issue that she'd been drinking and that she generally drank more than any of my friends' parents, as far as I could tell. I don't think she'd go into the shakes or anything and she has never blacked out as far as I know. But she's a little woman and she loves her gin, and, anyway, it wasn't a talk that went well. Her response was an unequivocal "How dare you. You don't question my behavior—ever."

The worst of it was that there was no other outlet for my frustration with her. My father always defended her; he still does. Both of them are in strong denial; I think they'll be in denial to the grave. Even when my youngest sister—who herself has had serious problems with my mother—when she divorced, Mom couldn't imagine that she had anything to do with my sister's pain. She refused to be accountable in any way.

My sisters and my father and mother were brilliant; everything came so easily to them. It was humiliating as the oldest girl, having to fight to get recognition, accolades. The bar was always being set higher and higher. But during my teenage years I worked my butt off and became a straight A student. It was never enough for my parents. Only after I earned my doctorate did they seem content.

The first time I saw a psychologist was in high school. I saw one once or twice, but I only faintly remember those meetings. I'm sure that I should have been going all along. I had self-esteem issues and I was obsessed with my weight. You never would have known it. I was popular. Most of the time I had friends, though not a lot of boyfriends.

But I always sensed that something was wrong. Once I cut myself on these little triangles. And I showed my mom, and she said, "Good for you, honey. You fixed it yourself." I mean, it makes no sense. I was like, don't you notice that this is a scream for help? In my mind, I couldn't have been screaming any louder. But in my family, unless you were bleeding and in crisis, you'd have to make do, because everyone was in a state of crisis. My parents were overwhelmed by their lives. And compared with my sisters, I looked good to them. I was a good kid. The only partying I did was getting high with one of my sisters when we went to walk the dog, and I did steal the little vodka bottles from the airlines now and then.

The story was the same in college, except that by then, I knew something was up and that it was serious. On one hand, I loved college. I went to the school that I wanted and I had all these friends, but on the inside, I felt this hole, this darkness. So I started seeing someone for depression and anxiety and that doctor put me on Valium. That's when I started taking pills.

But I was still depressed. I was still a great student, but now when I worked hard, I partied a little more. And then I worked even harder. It was that way with my weight, too. I think I was sort of a depressed eater. I'm short, so 10 pounds on me is everything. So if I was feeling heavy, I'd start working out like crazy. I'd train for marathons. I was always focusing on other things as the reasons that I was unhappy rather than on the abandonment issues that I was experiencing.

Then came Ethan, my first true love. My only college love. We met at the end of my freshman year, and I broke up with him about a year and a half later because he was afraid of commitment. Not long after that, he was diagnosed with leukemia. I dropped out of school for a few semesters to be with him at his parents' home in Santa Barbara. He died when I was 21.

It was then that my fear and anxiety really reached new heights. I'd been taking antianxiety medication for a couple of years by then but not massive amounts. But as I finished up school and entered graduate school, I went at both my studies and partying pretty hard. School was still the priority, and I was never a big drinker, but I was starting to experiment here and there, including with this person who wound up being my husband. Being with him, when we were dating, we did a lot of cocaine. And that didn't stop after we moved in together. At least, he didn't stop, which made me really angry. He would go out and not come home.

Eventually, he went into outpatient treatment, and I went with him as the enabler and codependent. And he did quit before we got married. I quit the coke entirely, too.

And then...the kids came along, and the migraines. I'd started having migraines when I was in graduate school, and I always struggled with them. We also had four kids in five years, beginning when I was 29, just a year after we'd wed. I wasn't using coke or pills during any of that time that I was pregnant, but as they all began to grow up, I began taking Xanax and Vicodin for the pain.

That's around the time my marriage started to unravel, too. The beginning of it was okay, although he pushed me down when I was pregnant once or twice. Then he became increasingly abusive verbally and mentally, and my occasional glass of wine went from little glass to a bigger glass to one of those zoo cups, and it went from an occasional glass to a daily drinking habit. It totally changed my behavior—all of it. By the time we'd been married for 15 years, I was angry and depressed. It was ugly. It took me far too long to understand how deeply angry and vengeful he is. There's no serenity there. He never went through any steps or had a sponsor or made amends to anyone. And the end of our marriage was just brutal. He cheated constantly, he quit working, he was demeaning, he turned the kids against me. We had this big fancy house where I still live with my kids, and we had the police here.

When I finally threw him out, I numbed myself with pills at the beginning of the process. But as we went through the divorce and a dispute over the children which resulted in shared custody, I lost weight and I started dating a younger guy who was very fun and a relief after what I'd gone through but who also reintroduced me to cocaine. It was so freeing and I kept saying to myself I'll stop when this custody thing is over. But it went on and it went on, and the time the kids were away I just thought I was going to die.

With my financial situation, things just spiraled out of control, because there was nothing to stop me. The custody fight dragged on for a year and a half, and I was buying ounces by myself. I went crazy.

Alexis's family tried to help. After a visit to her parents' home in Connecticut with her children—a visit during which the children misbehaved and her parents offered Alexis unsolicited parenting tips—Alexis decided that they would "never have a role" in her life "ever again." Highly concerned with her anger and sensitive to the very real possibility that she had become an addict, her parents soon after flew to her home in Albuquerque, where they met her at her house and staged an intervention. Alexis went grudgingly to the treatment facility where they had arranged to send her, but she was making calls to line up cocaine before she left the grounds less than a month later. As she says, "I just wasn't ready. I hadn't bottomed out."

When I went back to treatment the second time, I weighed 90 pounds. One of my sisters came to visit me soon after and thought I had an eating disorder—that I was anorexic or bulimic—but I didn't have an eating disorder. I was still a coke head. And I was getting worse by the week. I didn't have four kids in five years not to raise them. I went crazy when they weren't home, which was half of the time.

The thing is—and the reason I finally reached out for help—even when they were home, I wasn't seeing them. I was still using, and I was still having migraines—I think I just wasn't dealing with life and my body was just shutting down—so I was in bed all day. I couldn't even drive I was so messed up.

I was using to numb the pain of not having my kids, but then I couldn't function when I had them, and I didn't know how to get out. I tried putting pictures of them out in the places where I typically cut lines, but that didn't work. Nothing did. I was sneaking around all the time.

I finally called my sister Sarah, who's closest to me in age, and said, "I need help." She was so relieved. She'd been through rehab twice herself, and I think she'd been praying that I'd experience a breakthrough before I did myself or my family irreparable harm. The cavalry showed up the next day: Sarah, my brother-in-law, my father, and an addiction recovery consultant who had determined that I'd probably do best at Creative Care.

I couldn't tell you much about those first days to a week. It took me four days to detox. I remember having chills, the shakes. I remember lying in bed and moaning for several days. Apparently, I did an intake interview curled up in a ball on a chair. I later introduced myself to the therapist who'd conducted the interview; I didn't even remember him.

After detox, I was incredibly angry. I said I was in the wrong place. I was there voluntarily. But after a point, once I realized I didn't want to die and that I needed help, I went to a group session led by a longtime marriage and family therapist at Creative Care, and I remember that I just couldn't get enough. It was brutal and raw and good and necessary. He's really good at group therapy. And as someone who is trained, I really respected the way he treated people.

So I was ready to get better and get well, but that's hard to do in 30 days, so though I hemmed and hawed I stayed a second month, and when at the end of that second month, they asked if I wanted to stay one more and focus on repairing my relationship with my kids, I was defiant, but I did stay—not just that third month, but also a fourth and half a fifth, and the experience saved my life.

While with us, Alexis did go home twice as test runs. Unsurprisingly, she found those visits scary. In fact, what Alexis realized—as most patients in addiction recovery settings do—is that going home, on the heels of everything she had accomplished during her inpatient work, was much more frightening than anything that had preceded it. Thankfully, she made the very smart decision to continue her aftercare work at an advanced out-patient addiction group for professionals in Albuquerque.

I went there every week for two years. It was hard. Though the family part of it, with my kids, was wonderful, going back to my life was really challenging. I realized that there was nothing I hadn't done high, other than sleep. So it took me months and months to feel comfortable in my own skin again. I just slowly started doing more and more and was more present, and I kept thinking, If I can just get through one year, I can go through everything once—every holiday, every birthday, every anniversary. Then you get to one year, and you have to go another year.

Then one day, I just knew I was done. My therapist in Albuquerque knew it, too. It had gone from scary, to good, to better, to better, to better, to this is hard, to, this is life.

I'm still on Vistaril [an anti-anxiety medication], which helps. (I began taking it at Creative Care, where for a short time I was taking a couple of other antidepressants.) But more important, I've learned how to live through things and to breathe.

Anxiety does creep up now, and if I'm really honest, I may not like the way I feel. Right now, for example, I have a lot of fear around one of my children, who is struggling in her own way.

Really, it wasn't getting sober that was hard. It's living life sober that's hard. There are times that I think if I don't do something...I have to do something. When my daughter found herself in trouble recently, I paced for hours on end. I walked circles in my closet. It was just like an out-of-body experience. Then I called people and talked and talked.

The thing is, I try and breathe, because I hold my breath a lot. When I'm upset now, I know I have tools. Pausing is huge. Praying is huge. I'm not an alcoholic, but I go to AA meetings when I don't want to go. I call people. I deal with the present. I ask: What is my part here? What's the next, right thing? What can I do? AA has all these stupid slogans: One Day at a Time; First Things First. But I've tried to find one that doesn't work, and they all do.

Alexis was a tricky case. She obviously had a very messy marriage. She was very distressed, feeling as she did that she didn't really fit well into her own family, that they didn't recognize her intellect or hold her in high enough esteem. Indeed, it wouldn't be overstating things to say that she was histrionic when she arrived at Creative Care. I think everyone on staff can still remember the screams about how she didn't want to be in treatment again, that she just wanted to go home.

It didn't happen overnight, but the turning point for Alexis, and what really made a difference in her treatment was that at Creative Care, she was finally able to calm down and relax. What Alexis had missed before coming to us was how astonishingly chaotic her life had become. Her kids were in disarray. She wasn't coping with her divorce or the resentment she felt toward her husband, by whom she felt used. She was physically in shambles and contributing to the stress by spinning out of control with cocaine. She was so all over the place that she wasn't focusing on what really needed attention: Alexis.

It was so extreme that when she first arrived, we put her on several medications, including the mood stabilizer Lithium, the anti-depressant Effexor, and the anti-anxiety medication Vistaril, which she continues to take today. Alexis also began to attend group therapy sessions in the morning and afternoon, to meet with a primary therapist once a week, and to follow the rest of the program at Creative Care.

Alexis was suffering withdrawal. She showed physical and psychological symptoms. At Creative Care we had decided that the best way to help her come off the addictive drugs was with an anxiety-reducing drug. Ideally, the medication would have been nonaddictive, but we decided that the benefits of the anxiety-reducer outweighed the risk of possibly introducing an additional addiction for Alexis. We felt this step was crucial because her tolerance was so high that nonaddictive drugs would not have worked at this point. We were able to steady Alexis with the anxiety-reducing drug and she was then able to process the psychological therapy.

It was then, finally, that she was able to address both her chemical dependency, and the unresolved trauma she'd endured both as a child who wasn't given what she needed by her parents, and as a wife who suffered for years with a lack of trust and with anger.

❧

11

How Families Experience Addiction, and How They Can Help

AS MUCH AS ADDICTS struggle with their addictions, it's nearly as draining for the families who love them. The irony is that families are often the last to know that the problem is so extreme.

Families often make the mistake of trying to "save" or "rescue" their family member from the consequences of addiction. This is a black hole. Family members cannot play both role of loved one and drug counselor. When people take professional direction and it does not work the first time, they usually abandon the advice and revert back to their old way of behaving. And "their" way can be misleading. Who can argue with a mother or father who says that they know their child better than anyone? Who can argue with a spouse who believes their partner is incapable of lying? The truth is that when someone is in the throes of addiction they are not themselves. This is what family members usually deny—they cannot believe that their relative is capable of lying, cheating, and stealing money to pay their habit. It is very hard for family members to separate the person from the addictive behavior. Thus they enable addictive behavior.

The best thing that family members can do to help is to focus on what their loved one does, not on what they say. Family members need to reach out for help just as much as the person with addiction. ALANON is a good resource, as well as a family therapist who understands addiction.

Part of the reason is simple manipulation. Someone with an addiction problem has to lie about it. You can't keep it going if you're going to be frank about it.

Denial plays an equally big part in why families are often the last to know. I'm constantly amazed by the signs that mothers and fathers, sisters and brothers, and sons and daughters are willing to overlook because they don't want to admit that a loved one is an addict. The signs are usually there, in front of their eyes: alcohol on the breath, a sudden decrease in the ability to function at school or at work or at home, problems in relationships that don't entirely make sense, fatigue, reckless driving, endangering themselves and others, paying bills late or not at all, changes in friends, changes in overall attitude, sometimes even physical fights. Even faced with some, or sometimes all, of these things, family members continue to look the other way. Why? Because as long as they deny it, they don't have to face that there's a problem. If you don't recognize it, it doesn't exist. Some of the rationalizations we have heard include "I thought he used cocaine because it helped him concentrate," and "She drank because she was working hard to pay the bills and was under a lot of stress."

In most cases, family members enable the addict through denial because the truth hurts.

Sometimes denial has other motivations, however. Sometimes, for example, family members feel that it's easier to be around the alcoholic family member, for example, if the person is drinking because he or she is happier then. They try to convince themselves that there's no harm in indulging the addict. But there *is* harm; the addict does cross the line, hurting him- or herself and, in some cases, becoming physically or mentally abusive to others. Often only after an addict has done some real damage do family members shake themselves out of their denial to acknowledge the serious problem.

Sometimes family members are afraid to ask the hard questions. We've seen a number of children, for example, who worried about how their relationship with their mother or father would be impacted if they made their questioning overt. They wondered, Will Mom or Dad get angry? Individuals raised in a stressful, emotionally closed environment often legitimately fear the consequences of labeling someone an addict, so they do nothing until a catastrophic event forces their hand.

Unfortunately, denial also serves selfish ends. We had a patient several years ago married to an older, frail woman. She was exceedingly slow to acknowledge and confront his addiction because she too was a heavy drinker, and he supported her financially. Even when his sister successfully encouraged him to come to us for help, his wife was reluctant to get behind his recovery. She acknowledged later that she continued the fantasy that everything was normal because she worried that any disturbance of the status quo would put her life as she knew it at risk, that he might leave her.

But not every family lives in a state of denial about the addiction per se. Sometimes they unwittingly live in denial about the root cause of an addiction. In such cases—and we see many—the family doesn't understand the emotional undercurrents that are tearing apart their loved one until that person is in the throes of addiction.

Indeed, what I hear most frequently in letters from families is this: "We never understood what was going on. Thank you for taking the time to explain it to us." Very often the addict's family unwittingly plays a role in fueling the addiction. For example, when parents burden a child with unrealistic expectations, he may turn to drugs or alcohol out of distress over not living up to their ideals. Family members may rely on the addiction for their own psychological equilibrium. Perhaps they use the addict as an outlet for repressed rage. Parents or spouses may unconsciously relish the role of caretaker because it distracts them from their own emotional issues.

When family members have contributed to an addiction, family therapy can help expose and change this dynamic. Daniel, a patient of mine who suffered from bipolar disorder and smoked pot daily, received a letter from his father after he had been at the clinic for a couple of weeks. The letter said: "I know you'll find inner strength. We believe in you." Instead of bolstering his resolve, the letter enraged Daniel. He felt his parents loved to appear saintly, concealing their real anger and frustration toward him. In family therapy, the parents learned to express these negative emotions toward him constructively. Daniel then felt that their communication with him was becoming more genuine.

When someone has suffered from an addiction for a long time, the family dynamic adjusts to accommodate that addiction. If the addict recovers, relationships must shift, and this can be difficult, even alarming, for the family. As a result, they may unconsciously try to sabotage treatment. Often this attempt takes the form of a practical concern. For example, the mother of one of my patients insisted that the clinic wasn't in a safe neighborhood. Since she had little evidence for this assertion, unconscious fear of her daughter's recovery seemed to be behind it.

Similarly, when family members worry over the cost of treatment, they may exaggerate financial concerns due to unconscious anxiety about the patient's recovery. Practical concerns should be taken seriously, but it's important to recognize that anxiety about the patient's recovery may blow these concerns out of proportion.

I'll give you a more subtle example of how families unwittingly play a role in a loved one's addiction issues by introducing you to Nancy, whose daughter, Diane, gave her the surprise of her life when she overdosed on alcohol and prescription drugs.

NANCY'S AND DIANE'S STORY

When Diane was admitted to the emergency room at the Cedar-Sinai Medical Center in Los Angeles, Nancy was 3,000 miles away at home in Wilmington, North Carolina. She could barely process the news that Diane's best friend, calling from the hospital, was delivering. Nancy simply couldn't reconcile what she was hearing with the daughter she knew so well and whose judgment Nancy couldn't have trusted more. In Nancy's words:

> As a child, Diane was really easygoing, and very bright. As she grew older, she became interested in dancing and acting and she was really very talented in both. She was also a great student. And she was so popular. Her father and I have never socialized as much as Diane. She's just very sweet and loves people, and they love her. She was homecoming queen of her high school. She also became a runner-up in the Miss America pageant for the state of North Carolina. Anything she wanted to do, she could, and she did it well.

I was never the pushy mom. It was always her ideas, and when opportunities came up, I'd say: Do you want to do this? You don't have to do this. But she pressured herself because she had the ability to do all these things. I remember in high school, I thought she was overloaded with way too many things, but she handled them all.

It was her decision to go to L.A. and act when she graduated from college, and she did well with that, too, which was why it was a shock, a complete shock, when her friend Kim called to say Diane had overdosed. I'm not even sure on what anymore: Benadryl and alcohol and some other over-the-counter medication. I couldn't believe that it was an attempted suicide.

As it turns out, Diane was suffering—as my brother Mustafa had—from clinical depression. And like him, she had no idea. As her mood swings became more erratic—over a lost audition, a young studio executive who didn't call her for a second date—she began to drink for the first time in her life. As her emotional condition worsened, she began drinking more frequently, until it quickly become an addiction.

The news stunned Diane's family, but as they learned when Diane came to us and we embarked on a course of family therapy, addiction doesn't happen in a vacuum. Although Nancy couldn't have guessed that her daughter would turn to alcohol, she did unwittingly play a role in her suicide attempt, as did Diane's father.

Like when the word "alcoholic" came up, that was a total "what?" When did that happen? Diane never did much more than experiment with alcohol when she was younger. She might have had a drink here or there. She knew her grandparents

were alcoholics, but she'd never been around it because her
father and I don't drink.

What Nancy's family came to understand, through Diane's
therapy after the attempt, was that depression, not alcohol, was
the root problem.

It's how she started coping, though she had no idea that that's
what she was doing. I don't think depression was even in her
vocabulary at that point. And that's partly my fault. Her
father has suffered from depression during our entire marriage.
And it's something that I hid from my kids and shouldn't have.
But we're talking 30 years ago. I hid a lot of things, including
problem with finances, which I wish I had been more open
about.

I'm not sure when the depression started, and I don't know
if I understand everything she went through, but she has
described it as a dark feeling of hopelessness. I think it might
have been precipitated by dating. In high school, she had a dif-
ferent boyfriend every week. And as she grew older, she had
some boyfriends who were very nice and some who weren't so
nice. Sometimes from her apartment in L.A., she would call
me in the middle of the night, crying about a boyfriend. I'd
say, "Do you want to come home? You can always come
home." But she'd say, "No, this is where I want to be." But
she couldn't make any decisions. She didn't know what was
best for her at the time, which wasn't like her at all.

The hard thing for us was she was way out there and we
were in North Carolina. But also, I never suspected a serious
problem. I thought she was going through some initial separa-
tion anxiety, that she was finding her way. Even when she did
things that scared me—like moving from the home of a family

friend in Riverside to a friend's apartment in downtown L.A.
so she could be close to dance classes—I just trusted her deci-
sions. She'd never been in trouble.

Nancy believes she should have asked more questions and made herself more available to answer Diane's. She and her daughter have always been close, but she realizes there were things that Diane was afraid to ask her, possibly for fear she would hurt her mother's feelings.

Last summer, she had me go to the counselor she sees now because there were some issues she wasn't comfortable asking or talking about. One of those things she shared was her sadness over the fact that her dad was never happy, which sur-prised me. He functions very well, but he was emotionally detached, and she was very sensitive to that. I guess she thought it was her job to try and make him happy. But I missed all that. She wasn't really a daddy's girl. I didn't see that she val-ued his opinion as much or maybe even more than mine.

Diane has always been very empathic, too, and there were other things that gnawed at her about which I wasn't aware. My sister has bipolar disorder, which we also didn't know about for a long time. We just thought that she made bad choices and did weird things. And when Diane heard people talking negatively about her, she was very sensitive to their criticisms. But I didn't know it then. It came up in therapy, how Diane thought the family was unkind to my sister and didn't do enough to help her.

Today Diane, who spent four months with us, is enjoying a very successful recovery. It wasn't easy initially. Says Nancy, "I used to not know what areas I could ask about or what to say," but in the last few years, she adds that "we've gotten really open, and now we have very honest communication." Much of the family's progress is due to Diane's openness and perseverance. She is now working as a nanny and at a preschool—environments that have encouraged her to relate to how she felt as a child and have stimulated a number of productive conversations.

Diane is also lucky in that her mother is happy to attend the AA meetings that Diane so faithfully attends when visiting her daughter in Los Angeles or when Diane is home in North Carolina. That families can attend AA meetings, even without being members, is a wonderful thing. I wish more families would take an active role in the support groups to which their loved ones belong.

The biggest breakthrough, however, happened in the earliest stages of Diane's recovery. Nancy puts it best when she explains, "We had to talk about some hard stuff, and it was difficult for us, as it must be for all families. The thing is, once you get that stuff out of the way, the rest is easy."

BEYOND DENIAL

Another trap families fall into is what I call emotional leveraging. It's when a family member threatens the addict with severe consequences if he or she doesn't quit drinking or taking drugs.

We saw a situation recently when a husband whose wife had become addicted to painkillers told her that if she didn't kick the habit, he was going to leave her and take their three children with him.

DAVID'S AND MARTHA'S STORY

David loved his wife, Martha, but he had reason to worry about his family. Martha started taking the synthetic opiate Suboxone in order to relieve pain in her lower back. Suboxone, also prescribed to treat heroin addiction, is itself highly addictive; patients typically are prescribed only a one-month supply at most. A year later, Martha was *still* taking Suboxone. Often it takes family members a surprisingly long time to accept that something is very wrong.

Eventually, the reality of her addiction became inescapable to David. Still, Martha refused to admit the scope of the problem. She argued that she needed the drug to treat her back as well as her migraine headaches (which likely she had developed because of the Suboxone use; headaches are a frequent side effect). She also thought the drug made her less depressed, which it may have done.[1] Most important to David, Martha vigorously denied that she was addicted to the medication, despite the fact that she was obtaining her supply without a prescription over the Internet. In the meantime, she was paying less and less attention to the children and spending more time in their bedroom, alone, either asleep or drowsing.

To keep his sanity and gain insight into how to approach the problem, David began attending regular meetings at Al-Anon, a 12-step program of recovery for friends and family members of addicts. Around the same time, he began using their marriage and three children as leverage against Martha, who, after some coercion, reluctantly agreed to a stay at the Cirque Lodge in Sundance, Utah.

Cirque Lodge, as readers may know, is an excellent facility that tackles all manner of alcohol and drug addiction. But after nine days of confronting her addiction, Martha had had enough. She bought a plane ticket, packed her suitcases, and headed back home to Texas.

David was furious—and frustrated. When someone leaves a facility prematurely, it's a statement and a very bad sign that the person's addiction is becoming more chronic.

Again he threatened her. This time, however, the threats weren't empty, and both Martha and her family, who intervened, sensed as much. They discovered Creative Care online and convinced her to make the trip to California.

At first, it looked very much like she'd repeat her experience at Cirque Lodge. She repeatedly threatened to leave, saying that David was making a case for divorcing her and poisoning her children against her. She wanted to talk to her attorney. She felt that she was going crazy because she was in such a powerless state.

But she wasn't. As we pointed out to her, she was in charge. She could stay or she could leave. All we could do was negotiate with her, we reminded her. We essentially said to her, "Let's figure this out together. We're on your side. If you want to see David, let's invite him to see you. If you aren't ready to taper off your Suboxone intake, we'll wait until you are."

It was exactly what she needed to hear to turn the corner. Once we empowered Martha, she was able to take her first steps on the road to recovery. She had been reacting so much of the time that she lost sight of a realization she herself had made: that she needed help. In fact, within a week of putting the decision in her hands, Martha came to us and said that she was ready to slowly taper herself off the drug.

Martha wound up staying with us for a couple of months. As it happens, her father had grappled with alcoholism, but his addiction was never openly discussed and Martha was in such deep denial that she didn't think it affected her in any way. She was raised to believe the myth of functional alcoholism when, trust me, there is nothing functional about it. She had lived with a neglectful, abusive, and emotionally unavailable parent, and she was paying a price for it.

Yet by coming to terms with her childhood for the first time, she began to understand how her deep-seated anxieties had helped fuel her addiction. It was the second in a series of steps that I hope will take her to a lifelong recovery.

HOW FAMILIES CAN HELP

Intuition is the greatest tool a family has in helping a loved one overcome addiction. The family knows the addict better than anyone and can intuit when the person's behavior is off kilter. It is very hard to act on that intuition because a family's filters are set to blot out frightening possibilities.

The bonds that tie us can also blind us.

Addiction happens when someone develops a maladaptive way of adjusting. This fact is very hard for families to not only accept but understand. But there are ways to get involved; there are ways to help a loved one. It is critical to ask questions. We all make assessments when we enter a situation. If a scene doesn't seem right, if a loved one is acting strangely or in a way that raises red flags, find out why. If you aren't asking questions, then you are in denial, and you are culpable; you are enabling your loved one to self-destruct. You are part of the problem.

Be nosy. Maybe a loved one says that he or she only drinks on weekends. If you don't quite believe that, poke around. Maybe he *does* only drink on the weekends, but then he consistently drinks until he blacks out, which is alcoholic drinking. Do what you can to get an accurate inventory of what's being consumed. It's hard work—much harder than minimizing the situation, which is an easy trap to fall into. (At times even staff members minimize, because they want to believe their patients.) More important, don't take them at their word.

If addicts will lie to themselves, they will lie to you, too. Don't take it personally.

Listen. One of the biggest catalysts of the healing process is when a recovering addict is able to say to family members: "I'm so upset with you, Mom, for not protecting me from Dad," and the other things that he or she hasn't been able to say for one reason or another. It's not always possible for everyone to take part in a discussion of what they contributed to the problem. Nine times out of ten, the biggest perpetrator—the absentee parent, the abusive spouse—is no longer around. But patients always land in a much better place once they are able to put their feelings where they belong, before the people who most need to hear about them.

Last but not least, get involved. You might be surprised to learn that families can be just as resistant to recovery as patients. I can't tell you how often we encourage family members to go to Al-Anon meetings so that they can better understand what they should and shouldn't do to help a loved one's recovery. Yet they don't want to be imposed on, or else they are embarrassed by the prospect of discussing their very personal experience with people they don't know. I empathize. But I cannot stress enough that it is much easier to understand the severity of the situation and to become educated about the recovery process if you are a part of it. As I tell my patients' families, learning about addiction and medication is just as important as learning about any other condition, such as diabetes or anemia or cancer.

Because addiction is so complicated and there is so much to learn—about setting boundaries, not contributing to codependency, and, often how to address addicts with a heavy trauma history—the more that family members undertake to understand and help a loved one, the better that person's chances of an enduring recovery.

12

Staging the Intervention

*I*NTERVENTIONS, AS YOU MAY know, are attempts by family members, friends, and sometimes even colleagues to convince addicts that they need to get professional help before their addiction kills them. Interventions are by no means the only way that addicts come to arrive at treatment facilities. In fact, I'd say that less than 10 percent of the patients we see at Creative Care arrive on the heels of an intervention. More often, our patients are driven by legal trouble, or serious emotional issues, such as panic attacks after using a lot of drugs, or—more often than you might think—because they recognize that they are in trouble.

Why aren't interventions as common in fact as they are in the popular imagination? I suspect it's because while interventions can be very effective, they can also be abominations that make addicts feel ambushed rather than supported. In truth, I feel that whether they work boils down to the interventionist and timing, and you never really know how good either is until you stage the intervention.

ORIGIN OF INTERVENTIONS

Vernon Johnson, a recovering alcoholic who organized a church study group in Minneapolis in the early 1960s, is credited with coining interventions. His group tried to find ways to encourage alcoholics to help themselves before they hit rock bottom. They concluded that, in most cases, it couldn't be done—that most alcoholics are on a suicide mission, whether they know it or not—so they came up with the concept of an intervention.

The concept hasn't changed much over the years, and as you probably know from watching one on television, if not in life, it works like this: The addict's family and friends come together—sometimes clergy and an employer are involved, too—and they give the individual a reality check. (Anyone included in the intervention should have firsthand knowledge of the addict's problem. And the group can't include anyone who has an active chemical dependency problem.)

At the same time as the group confronts the addict, they make the person aware that he or she can live a different kind of life, one free from the physical and emotional pain and aloneness that nearly all alcoholics endure.

But this little ecosystem of loved ones doesn't operate on its own, with the model of Johnson, who puts a great deal of emphasis on technique. Indeed, Johnson strongly advocated that loved ones work with a trained professional to confront the addict and lay down the terms by which that person must abide (generally that includes entering a treatment program), as well as the consequences of not meeting those terms.

The interventionist helps them decide in advance how to approach the individual, what their tone should be, and what facility best suits the person's needs.

That last part of the process involves a number of practical questions, such as whether the addict has insurance to defray the cost of treatment and what the insurance company's requirements are. If public funding is necessary, the group, with the interventionist's help, can find out what local agency authorizes treatment. (If the family has the financial resources to pay for treatment, the options broaden considerably, including whether to turn to an inpatient or outpatient addiction treatment program. Obviously, I'm biased, but I do believe that inpatient residential treatment is far more effective than outpatient treatment when dealing with addiction and emotional issues. My experience is anecdotal, but even healthcare information provider Medstat has published studies demonstrating that residential stays of 28 days are nearly twice as effective in preventing relapse as stays of less than 7 days.)

HOW IT WORKS

In Johnson's model, interventions are straightforward. Step 1 is for every participant to write a letter to the addict, explaining why they are all getting involved and what they they will do—or not do—if their overture is rejected.

The second step is for the interventionist to review the letters and to start planning the logistics of the treatment that is being proposed.

The intervention takes place during the third step. Interventions aren't terribly long: They typically last from 15 to 30 minutes. They are short meetings because they are not dialogues or negotiations. Rather, during the intervention, the addict listens to each person read his or her letter. The interventionist then explains the treatment program that has been arranged. Soon afterward, the addict decides to go—or not to go.

BUT DOES IT WORK?

Over the years, many addiction experts have come to conclude, as I have, that interventions are hit or miss. I do think they offer many benefits—including benefits to the family and friends who are trying to help their loved ones. After all, interventions are caring ways to point out a loved one's devastating behavior and communicate what you, as a family member, are willing to support. If you've been watching, powerlessly, from the sidelines, a intervention also is an opportunity to say what you need to say, including that you're no longer willing to look the other way. Some people go so far as to consider an intervention successful as long as the family or other loved ones who intervened feel they did the right thing and are then able to move forward in their own lives. (I happen to disagree.)

Others see interventions as intrusive and damaging at worst and ineffective at best. And while I hate to say it, many addicts go to treatment expressly to get their friends and families off their backs.

A forced intervention—and the time subsequently spent at a treatment facility—can anger an addict, so much so that he or she is in even worse condition than before the intervention.

I can see both sides of the argument, but the bottom line is that I don't believe interventions are as promising as once believed. Partly that owes to outsize expectations. Partly it owes to a cultural shift. When they were first introduced, interventions were typically orchestrated around a high-functioning alcoholic: someone with a job and a family and a great deal of motivation to right his or her destructive course. But not all addicts fall into that category. Some are simply incapable of helping themselves. Moreover, as families have become more fragmented geographically, fewer addicts have the kinds of deeply involved families as they did in the early 1960s, when the concept was introduced. Further, I fundamentally believe that most addicts are already emotionally frail, and they don't respond well to being in the center of what can easily become a family argument.

That said, if an intervention *is* decided on, I strongly prefer a more positive approach, one that says to the addict: It's us addressing this problem together. You're not alone.

CHOOSING AN INTERVENTIONIST

Most interventionists aren't clinicians. Most are in recovery themselves, so they know about denial. They know the havoc that addicts can wreak on a family. They know about codependencies within families. So they have knowledge and wisdom and experience and insights into addiction. This is a very good thing. In fact, when interventions do work, there's no question that a good interventionist was involved, which is why it's important to choose one carefully.

What should you consider? As I've said, an overly aggressive intervention can alienate the addict, to the extent that he or she ends up drinking or using drugs even more. A confrontational style is especially dangerous if the addict has a serious psychiatric condition. For schizophrenics, for example, such an approach can be very frightening and even potentially trigger a violent episode.

Sophisticated interventionists also don't impose rigid game plans on the proceedings; instead they let family dynamics shape the intervention. (For instance, after meeting with a family, they can identify who might break down and bargain with the addict—the person who might say "Okay, maybe you don't have to go to treatment if you can just stick to one or two drinks a night"—and weed out that potential saboteur.)

And good interventionists act as facilitators. Rather than dominate the intervention, they let the addict's loved ones do the talking. (In all likelihood, even if the addicts resist the intervention, they prefer receiving advice from people they know rather than from a stranger who has been imposed on them.)

Last, besides focusing on the addict, a skilled interventionist will encourage the whole family to change, helping them to recognize enabling and provoking behaviors.

JASPER'S STORY

Despite my skepticism of the general efficacy of interventions, they can, as I've mentioned, work. Jasper was a patient of ours who came to Creative Care through an intervention, and I believe it saved his life.

Jasper is a serious, intelligent young man from the Pacific Northwest, with thick brown hair and a wiry build. Like many of the people whose stories you've read in this book, Jasper comes from a loving family. He had a safe home environment. He was never deprived of anything that he could recall. But when he arrived at our door, he'd been terribly unhappy for as long as he could remember. He was filled with self-loathing, he felt detached from his parents, and he despised authority figures. He was also using crack cocaine.

Jasper was smart enough to understand that he was atypical. He was also savvy enough about his own wrecked state that when his parents eventually staged an intervention to get him help—using a trained interventionist—he didn't fight them. He let them send him to us.

It was a transforming experience. Not only did the intense psychotherapy sessions in which he participated provide startling insights into why he was unhappy, but Jasper took away tools to stop the destructive thought patterns in which he had always indulged. He also learned to love himself, at long last.

When I was born, in Portland, Oregon, I weighed in at a scrawny 2 pounds 6 ounces. I was five weeks premature and didn't have the use of my lungs, so there was a big concern that I'd have brain damage, though that never did become apparent.

I'm an only child. My parents had me pretty late. My mom had miscarried once before I arrived, and I guess they decided that one child was enough—that there was too much of a chance of more going wrong.

My parents were the most loving, kind, and hardworking people I've ever known. My dad headed up a broadcasting company and my mom was an accountant. But they were very involved in their work, so I raised myself. And I didn't have a lot of friends growing up. I was the kid who went to grade school a year after everyone else my age started.

When a lot of kids were doing "normal" social things like experimenting with drinking and girls, I was more into computers and reading and writing and things that were very solitary. And I liked to stay home. I was a misfit, basically. I never did go to any dances or to prom. My friends and I would hang out and play video games instead.

When the time rolled around for me to go to college, I decided on Lewis & Clark in Portland. I'd started working as a barista at Starbucks my senior year and didn't want to quit. And my closest friends were younger and still local, so I wanted to stay in town. But again, I felt like I didn't fit in at college. I was from Portland, unlike most of the students. And because I was raised to be careful around alcohol—my mom's parents had both been alcoholics—I wasn't partying, unlike everyone else.

After about a year, I just told my parents: I'm going to drop out of college. I'm not ready. I'm wasting your money. I don't know what I want to do. I'm going to just work, and live with my friend Jason, and figure out what I want to do.

And that's what happened. I moved into an apartment with Jason, and for a couple of years, I just worked and went out and had coffee with friends. Everything was great. But as I started getting closer to the age where I should have been graduating and wasn't, I started to feel more and more like an alien again. I felt I wasn't moving forward whereas my friends gradually were. But I was paralyzed by fear. I didn't know what I wanted to do. I had ten ideas that were competing for my attention and nothing was getting done.

Around this time, Jasper was diagnosed with bipolar disorder, after beginning to see a counselor again to discuss his erratic mood swings and what he has called his "deep, deep depressions." He was given medication, which helped—for a while.

My parents wanted to help and didn't know what to do, so I said, "We have a little money. Houses in Portland are cheap but getting more expensive. How about if we buy a beat-up house in the city as an investment, and I'll live there and fix it up," and they did that.

Once in the house, though, it was sort of more of the same. The big difference was that because it was spacious, some of my friends came to live with me and to throw parties, including for my twenty-first birthday, when we had a huge party with around 250 people.

It was a big night for me and I sort of thought: I can try this drinking thing. I can be legal and responsible and it will be okay. Also, I'd started seeing a girl who I really liked a lot—the only girl who, it seemed, had shown any attraction to me whatsoever.

That night I drank four gigantic gin and tonics. A lot of my friends there were really hammered. I drank until four or five in the morning. And finally I slept with this girl, which was a great thing for me. It hadn't been long before then that I'd actually kissed a girl for the first time, so this was a very big deal.

And for a short while, I felt normal. I had my routines. I worked, came home, saw her. Then I learned that she slept with a really good friend of mine at the same time that we were dating. I have an obsession with the ultimate romantic ideal, and that really messed me up. I literally wanted to die.

I knew I couldn't blow my brains out—that that wasn't socially acceptable. So I started to drink a lot. And by a lot, I mean every day for six months. I was in a steep downturn until I became romantically involved with another girl, a friend of a friend, and I felt like I didn't need to die anymore. But after about a year, girl number two left me, and after pretending to be happy about that for about a week, I started drinking really heavily again.

The next couple of years were pretty ugly. I sat in my house and mostly drank and grew my beard. I spent every day drinking and every day drunk. I can barely remember that period.

Drugs found their way in there, too—mostly pills, weed. When I was feeling really self-destructive, I'd get a gas can and a rag and shove that in my face. I figured it was a good way to kill brain cells.

By this point, people were saying Jas, maybe you should knock it off. They weren't terribly serious about it though, and I wasn't serious about it. And basically I met another girl—and this was really good. We both drank, but one day after a couple of occasions when I got too drunk and said and did things that I shouldn't have—yelling at her, almost tantamount to verbal abuse; I often had emotional outbursts when I was drunk—she told me she didn't want anything to do with me because I was an alcoholic and her father was an alcoholic who had died slowly on dialysis.

I couldn't take it. After the breakup, I went to the drug dealer who I bought weed from and said, "What can I buy that will fuck up my life and kill me as quickly as possible?" and he gave me crack cocaine. And I did it. I pretty much became the guy who sits in his basement and drinks and does drugs and listens to records. I was just waiting to die. This went on for two or three months. My body and my brain were just in terrible shape.

All this time, I was still taking meds for my bipolar, but you're not supposed to drink and take medication and while I battled with that—trying to do one and then the other—the medication was losing the battle, and so was I. This is how bad things were: I remember waking up one day in the basement. I'd been drinking a lot the night before, and I wanted to drink something in the morning. All I could find were two half-drunk beers with mold growing inside them, and I drank them anyway. I puked my brains out afterward.

All this time, I thought my parents didn't know about what I'd been doing. Mostly I tried to avoid them so they couldn't see me, and when I went to their house, I thought I faked things pretty well.

I was wrong. They invited me over for Christmas dinner; I remember I had half a bottle of Maker's Mark whiskey for breakfast. And when I walked into their living room, everyone I love was there, telling me they didn't want me to die.

Frankly, I wasn't so scared of dying, but I didn't want to be the person I'd become for the next 30 years. What I really wanted was to stay with my parents. Live with them for a week, dry out, then return to life. But through the interventionist they'd hired, they already had plans in motion to send me to rehab at Creative Care because of its focus on dual diagnosis.

It's funny to say now, but I wasn't thinking at all about therapy I was going to get, but it's what really saved my life. I wound up staying for five months.

It's hard to capture the effect the treatment had on me. The truth is that I'd feel gung-ho about it one day, then jaded the next. I cycled a lot, trying to find the balance in my situation.

But there I came to understand myself much better than I ever had. The counselors there thought, for example, that the first six months of my life had an impact on me that I never before contemplated, that I suffered preverbal trauma from being disconnected from human contact at such a crucial time. And the fact is that I've never felt very grounded in my surroundings, or very attached to my mother, whom I feel very close to but more in a friendly way that's sort of hard to describe. Whether or not all of it is true, I'll never know, but you do hear a lot in AA that the formative years have a lot to do with how you cope as an adult, and I believe that that's right to a degree.

I also realized through so much time in group and individual therapy at Creative Care that when someone leaves you, you don't react in insanely astronomic ways. I came to understand how that whole aspect of me was a defense mechanism because of all the things I'd gone through when I was young, and no one seemed to do much about what I was going through. I mean, I was this kid who was totally alone and angry. And I learned in therapy that it was perfectly okay to be furious and that what was I was feeling was a perfectly rational response to what was going on in my life at the time.

I also worked through a lot of relationship stuff finally. I realized it was okay to be vulnerable and not to assume that everybody was fucked and things would get screwed up. It was really tough, because it was one of those situations where, for a very long time, I was more comfortable with putting people at a distance and saying "fuck you," and not getting comfortable with people on a personal level. It was sort of like, I don't need to recognize you as a human being and can ignore you, but if you're my friend, I want more than anything for you to stick around.

I wouldn't say the therapists at Creative Care employed any new techniques, but they did teach me a whole lot about increasing my awareness of what I was doing; they taught me about contrary reactions.

They also put me on the right medication for bipolar, which I hadn't been taking. (I take lithium now, along with a mild antidepressant.) And I came to terms with the fact that I have to take these for the rest of my life, which I hadn't been able to do before I went into treatment.

Today, a year after getting out of treatment, I consider myself able to move forward in my life and able to grow. I wasn't able to grow for a long time because I was so terrified of

*taking any risks, so terrified of rejection that wasn't tangible.
I can finally be a human. I don't want to die on a daily basis.*

*I still think I'm a huge work in progress—I still crave pot
and uppers and downers; it's still hard for me not to think of
those things in a positive way—but if I hadn't gone into treatment, who knows what would have happened to me?*

*More important to me is that I can handle things now,
which is huge. When I'm upset, I write in my journal. I walk
around—a lot. I watch a movie. I try to focus on productive
things instead of myself and my anger, and it usually goes
away. That's the thing about emotions. They're temporary. I
thought they were permanent.*

INTERVENTIONS IN REVIEW

Professional interventions aren't for every family or for every
situation, as I've mentioned. The decision to orchestrate one
should be made carefully and with the advice of an experienced
counselor because there are so many risks attached.

The inescapable fact is that when an intervention fails, as it sometimes does, the failed effort can tear a family further apart. More,
many addicts can't be helped until they reach the point of asking for
help on their own. Though a confrontation may put addicts in
the frame of mind to accept help, if they're really not there yet,
intervention can create a lot of resentment down the road.

Of course, there aren't a lot of options when a loved one's
addiction issues have progressed to the extent that he's become a
danger to himself. Sometimes intervention can be a life-saving
choice and that sometimes makes the effort worthwhile.

13

The Risk of Waiting
Too Long

*T*HE RECEIVED WISDOM ABOUT recovery is that addicts need to be ready to take steps toward sobriety. According to one school of thought within clinical psychology, this readiness must ripen internally inside the individual for him or her to be able to cooperate with the recovery process. Yet I have seen patients enter my care that had been ready for treatment long before.

The challenge of treatment is figuring out how to help patients help themselves toward the threshold of health.

To explain this, I will focus the spotlight on one of the more complicated individuals whom we have had the honor of helping at Creative Care.

CHRISTOPHER'S STORY

Christopher, like Elizabeth—whom you met earlier in the book— spent his entire adult life plagued by bipolar disorder, but he was completely unaware of his condition. As I mentioned earlier, that's not uncommon. About 5.7 million American adults, or just less than 3 percent of the population age 18 and older in any given year, have bipolar disorder.[1] It usually develops in one's late teens or in early adulthood, and that's exactly when it struck Christopher.

Finding the offending genes is an ongoing endeavor for scientists, but brain-imaging studies are helping them determine where things go wrong in the brain to produce the condition and other emotional issues. Already there is evidence from imaging studies that strongly suggests that the brains of individuals with bipolar disorder differ from the brains of those who are healthy.

As we await more research and improved science, there are many ways to identify bipolar disorder, most notably dramatic mood swings: highs and lows known as episodes of mania and depression.

Unfortunately, sometimes another way to recognize bipolar disorder is if it is tied to substance or alcohol abuse. Many estimates place the percentage of people who are bipolar *and have alcoholism or substance abuse struggles* at a whopping 30 to 60 percent because they attempt to self-medicate. Consider the symptoms and it's easy to understand why. Signs of a manic period, for example, include extreme irritability, aggressive behavior, and racing thoughts. Signs of a depressive period are even worse: They include feelings of sadness, hopelessness, worthlessness; loss of interest in sex; fatigue; either oversleeping or an inability to sleep; and suicidal thoughts.

The problem, of course, is that while drugs or alcohol might provide temporary escape from the highs and lows associated with bipolar disorder, that relief is short-lived, so a person winds up using more and more in an effort to feel better longer and, ultimately, digs him- or herself into a hole out of which it's very hard to climb.

Unfortunately for Christopher, who began self-medicating by drinking heavily as a teenager, it would take more than two decades for anyone to diagnose his bipolar disorder. By then, he'd been a raging alcoholic for a long, long time.

I was born into a typical suburban situation in Cleveland, Ohio; we could walk to elementary school, which had a big playground. We were surrounded by parks. We played the games kids play, like cowboys and Indians.

My father was distant, emotionally and phsyically. He traveled quite a bit for work, so when he was home he was usually very tired and rather than play with us, he'd come home and have a drink and eat dinner with my mom while us kids ate separately.

When I was a little older, I went away to prep school in Pennsylvania—a coat-and-tie sort of place that my dad had attended. I was very quiet at first; it was a difficult period because I was really shy as a kid.

Then, like a lot of my peers, I began to drink, except I always seemed to drink more than most people, and I seemed to enjoy it more than others. I remember the first time I drank beer, my roommate had this whole theory about alcoholism. He said: Do you really enjoy it? That's when you know you're an alcoholic. Maybe the seed was planted then, but I remember thinking later on that I fell into that category.

I continued drinking a lot when I started as a freshman at Columbia as I turned 18. The transition was tough, having to meet all new people, but I was determined to make the best of it, and drinking helped.

At that point, I wasn't thinking about alcohol as a problem. Everyone had said that you have to party in college. So I did.

It took its toll. My junior year at college, I was put on academic probation. My parents, who'd announced to me earlier in the year that they were divorcing, worried that I was reacting to that news. That might have been the case. Even though I didn't necessarily have a close relationship with my dad, my parents had always seemed happy together and I was worried about my mom being on her own.

But I was also becoming depressed over other things that don't sound important now but were weighing very heavily on me at the time, like that I'd imagined that there would be a lot of sex in college, but there really wasn't, maybe because I was drinking a lot every night.

In fact, I was generally a failure with girls. My first real depression had to do with a breakup with a girlfriend in high school. I just remember being so despondent and feeling so much despair that I drank half a bottle of vodka. I really felt like I wanted to die.

Anyway, more and more, I'd deal with heavy intense negative stuff by drinking it away. I thought that was the macho, masculine thing to do. I even screwed up a Wall Street internship that my dad arranged for me because I kept calling in sick, I was drinking so much.

I couldn't handle school, either. When it came time for my Buddhism midterm, I sort of started writing my own religion in this blue book, which I didn't turn in. Instead, I walked out of the class in the middle of the test. This feeling of needing to just

*get out overwhelmed me suddenly, so unbeknownst to my
parents, I withdrew from school and went to live with my
kid brother for a while in Charlottesville, where he was going
to the University of Virginia.*

As is apparent, Christopher was becoming unable to finish
anything he started. But his inability to commit to college was
only the beginning.

Christopher was very much in an existential vacuum. He'd
been very depressed and drinking for a long time, and he was
becoming increasingly lost in this abyss. As we would later discover at Creative Care, Christopher had very low self-esteem and
low-grade depression. He didn't find any purpose in his family.
And though he envisioned greater things for himself, the alcohol
made it increasingly difficult for him to focus on anything mean-
ingful; as things failed to pan out for him, it caused him to sink
even further into a state of distress.

*I needed the break, but I withdrew more and more. My parents
wrote it off as my still having trouble with their divorce. But
I also had no idea of what I wanted to do after college.*

*The drinking escalated to a really high point during that
period, even with my brother around. I remember he went out
of town and I had the place to myself and I drank. I thought I
wouldn't get so drunk. I had a six-pack and told myself that I
was going to limit myself. But I had a Chinese dinner and that
six-pack, then I finished a 100-proof bottle of whiskey. And
I felt like I needed to get even more so I went to a few college
bars.*

*What I remember after that is landing in a seedy club and
talking to a server who kissed me on the lips, and that's last thing
I remember except for a vague conversation with a policeman,*

then of being in the backseat, where I was trying to pull apart handcuffs and broke my own arm. Then I remember being in the hospital, talking to doctors.

That's when my family first intervened. That was the impetus for my first trip to rehab. I went to a 30-day program in Indianapolis that my brother had found through a friend, and it worked for a while.

I moved back from Charlottesville into my dad's house in Cleveland, which he kept after my parents split, and I stayed sober. I did aftercare, too. But I didn't get a really good sponsor and I was really angry that I couldn't drink anymore. And at some point, my dad, who still traveled constantly, sold his house, too, so I moved to a little apartment.

On his own, Christopher's state became terribly fragile again.

I was doing little temp jobs, including working at a dialysis clinic, which wound up hiring me full time after a week. But after a year's time—everyone had said "Give it a year, give it a year"—I wasn't feeling any better. So with all kinds of fear, I started drinking again, and very quickly I was getting drunk every night on beer and whiskey in my tiny little apartment. Life was pretty miserable. I was sort of like a nurse's assistant at the clinic. But the dialysis stuff was pretty intense. Patients would die and I'd have to call the paramedics to come, and there was lots of blood and vomit and shit, and it wasn't a very pleasant place, so I felt like I deserved my drink. Also, my social life was limited. I'd do things with people from work but pretty much, I'd come home and get drunk.

Christopher, who felt he was starving spiritually, began attending Episcopal services at a nearby church. There he met a theology

teacher named Lucas James who would have a greater impact on
Christopher than he could have imagined.

*For a good long time, I was working and drinking and
spending time with the same small circle of friends who I didn't
let know me very well. Then I met Deborah, a woman who
used to come into a bookstore I frequented and who I fell for.
It was the first time I'd gone crazy over someone in years and
years. But after we fooled around a little bit and she dropped
her boyfriend, she changed her mind and went back to him.
And that's kind of when things really went off the rails. I
became really suicidal for the first time in my 30s. That's when
I bought a gun, and bullets, though I never put them in the
gun. It was just comforting to have.*

*Lucas, who could see how distraught I'd become, suggested
I start seeing his therapist, who really helped me. And life sort
of resumed, with me working and dropping by the liquor store
every night because I had to have at least a bottle of whiskey
and some beer.*

*I was longing for a woman, though, and about six months
later, I became involved with a young girl who worked at the
liquor store. She knew how much liquor I was buying every
day, but I think she romanticized what an alcoholic was.
Either way, for first time in a long time, I was smoking and
drinking less. It was one of the only times that I recall feeling
really, blissfully happy as an adult.*

*Things didn't work out for more than a couple of months,
though, and coming on the heels of that breakup with
Deborah, I didn't handle it well. I started to come apart at the
seams again, drinking, smoking pot, crying, feeling alone and
suicidal. I knew the thing was to reach out to other people, so
the weekend after she left, I called my boss and talked to him*

for an hour. I also called my mom, who until that point thought I'd been sober since that rehab stay. It was pretty terrible. Then a friend of my brother came down from Chicago to check on me and apparently I was dancing around naked in my apartment when he came. He took me to the hospital. I thought maybe we were going to a party. Then at the hospital they put me in their psych ward.

It was really straight out of One Flew Over the Cuckoo's Nest.

Soon enough, though, my mom came and gathered me up and took me to stay with her for a couple of months, which was nice. But eventually, it was time for me to move back to my apartment, and I did without any clear plan other than to see my therapist, and she was on vacation when I arrived. I used that as an excuse to start drinking again.

I had no job at this point—my boss at the dialysis clinic made it clear that they didn't want me back. My mother, who would have given me money, refused because I was open about continuing to drink. My dad wanted to help me but he insisted on my putting together a budget, but I couldn't do that because then they'd know how much I was drinking. I was low, very low. I started looking for answers, for a higher power. I'm compulsive by nature, so in addition to the old habits I'd gone back to, I became very excited about taking new theology classes at Lucas's seminary. I was still drinking every night but going to class and writing my papers, and everything held together for a while. But I began doing all-nighters on papers, then drinking myself into oblivion afterward. I couldn't do the papers at the end, and I got extensions and still couldn't do them. Then I just stopped going to seminary. Then I stopped going anywhere other than the liquor store. I was staying as drunk as I could while barely leaving the apartment.

That's when I became the most suicidal I've ever been. All I was doing was writing suicide notes. I thought I was running out of money. I kept taking out my gun and putting bullets into it and taking them out. Every night felt like my last night on earth. I continued to talk with my therapist but I couldn't drive to see her so we'd meet on the phone. Eventually I couldn't even make the call to her that I was supposed to make.

I'm not sure how long I lasted like that. A month or so, I think.

Finally, on a Saturday morning, I resolved to kill myself. I had my gun loaded and I kept picking it up and putting it down and I finally picked it up and held it up, underneath my chin, and was prepared to pull the trigger when, suddenly, there was this little sparrow on my porch that was yapping and yapping and yapping. We had little sparrows when we were kids, and I took this little sparrow as a sign that that Saturday wasn't the right day. The next day—this was June—it was Father's Day, so I didn't even get the gun out.

Then there was the Monday after Father's Day. All day long, it was like, I'll just have one more cigarette and I'll do it. But I just couldn't do it, which brought more despair.

I decided I was going to drink to work up the courage. (I used to drink to pay my bills, take out the trash, do laundry, make unpleasant phone calls; I got very energized when I drank.) Monday afternoon gave way to night, and again I resolved to finish what I'd started. I was sitting on the floor cross-legged with the gun under my chin again, pointing upward. And I stayed like that for some time, trying to muster the courage to pull the trigger, and the doorbell started ringing and it was Lucas. My therapist had broken her vow of confidentiality and asked him to check on me and it all felt so supernatural, his timing.

Christopher later said that he would have opened the door only for two people that night: his mother and Lucas, who very possibly saved Christopher's life.

> My therapist and my parents immediately decided that I needed urgent care and, in a rough way, that's how I ended up at Creative Care, where I was finally diagnosed with bipolar I disorder. It was so anticlimactic, as the doctor talked us through what it is and what the diagnosis meant. I think we were all shocked that no one had spotted it sooner. I knew I didn't feel entirely "normal," but I always chalked it up to just being depressed about my life.

It's important to note here that Christopher differed from Elizabeth, who suffered from bipolar II disorder. The distinction lies in the acuteness of the conditions, with bipolar II being the less severe of the two. The classic form of bipolar I disorder involves recurrent episodes of mania and depression and can, in worst cases, escalate into psychosis; people like Elizabeth with bipolar II disorder have episodes of manic behavior. Although both forms of the illness can begin with a mild depression at first—the average age at onset is 21—bipolar I disorder typically progresses to a severe form of mania, and nearly everyone who endures a single manic episode will have more of them.

Indeed, people who go without treatment typically experience about eight episodes of increasingly more severe manias and depressions, which can last from two weeks to half a year, over the course of their lives.[2] (It's no surprise, then, that Christopher grew so dramatically worse over time, even as his circumstances would seem far from adverse to someone without his condition.)

Bipolar I disorder affects both sexes in equal proportions, and it's thought to affect between 3 and 5 percent of the population globally.[3] In fact, it's the third leading cause of death for people between the ages of 15 and 24, and carries a 15 percent risk of suicide if left untreated. So Christopher's suicidal fantasies were not at all unusual for someone struggling with his particular issue.

THE END OF AGONY

Like many patients, when Christopher arrived at Creative Care, he thought he'd stay a month and get out. His plan, after that, was to get a gun and finish himself off. Like many patients, he also resisted medication initially. In fact, it was only after he experienced a hypomanic period—painting, journaling, jumping into the pool—that the staff, with the ready help of Christopher's family, was able to convince him that he needed to at least try medication. We began by first administering Paxil, then Geodon, and, later, Depakote.

Paxil is a trade name for paroxetine, an antidepressant in a group of drugs called selective serotonin reuptake inhibitors (SSRIs) that work to restore balance to chemicals in the brain that may be imbalanced. (Paxil is one of the most widely prescribed antidepressants in the United States. It was first approved by the Food and Drug Administration [FDA] in 1992.) Paxil is used to treat not only bipolar disorder but also anxiety disorders, posttraumatic stress disorder, and depression, among other things.

Geodon, meanwhile, is a trade name for ziprasidone, an antipsychotic medication used to treat both schizophrenic and bipolar patients, who can, in extreme cases, also suffer from hallucinations. It's much newer, having been approved by the FDA in 2001.

Last, Depakote—a brand of valproic acid, or valproate—is an anticonvulsant medication that was first approved by the FDA in

1983 for epilepsy and approved 12 years later to treat the manic
episodes associated with bipolar disorder. It works by boosting an
inhibitory transmitter called gamma-aminobutyric acid (GABA), a
chemical that carries messages between brain nerve cells. GABA
suppresses the transmission of certain nerve signals, which is
critical to rapidly stabilizing acute mania.

The combination worked. Says Christopher:

> Right away, I had more energy, and I started sleeping at night
> and I started to feel more normal. I also started working out
> with a trainer and swimming every day and even taking an
> acting class in town—someone from the staff would drive me.
> I basically resigned myself to staying however long they
> thought I needed to stay.

It wasn't simply as if a switch had been pulled. It took time, but
Christopher gradually began to rebalance.

> I was still in a really dark place for about nine months. I'd still
> have periods of just sleeping and sleeping and sleeping. But I
> finally found an Alcoholics Anonymous sponsor who I really
> connected with and still have today; I started getting a dif-
> ferent feel for Alcoholics Anonymous. I also began gaining
> confidence from my acting class.
>
> Really, there was a major shift after those nine months.
> I think that's when the meds—which I'm still taking—finally
> kicked in. I just began a different phase. I started to feel
> more comfortable with my therapists at Creative Care. I
> finally felt safe.
>
> Today I'm in sober living now and driving, which before
> was a huge deal for me. Before getting help, even when I was
> sober I was a wreck in the daytime.

I also see a therapist three times a week and I feel good about AA and go to meetings regularly, though I really lost the desire and the necessity to drink during my stay at Creative Care. I don't think about drinking very much at all.

Overall, I'm just much happier than I ever thought I'd be. I'm not freaked out by the same things. I feel grounded. I'm even doing improv now at a small club in town on occasion. I have a lot to be thankful for now.

CLEAN WHEN READY

Christopher is an example of an addicted individual who waited too long to get help. He was struggling with a lot of demons, and he took many detours before reaching a point where he realized he could no longer go it alone. Then he was ready. And many therapists will tell you that that is the only time addicts can reach sobriety—when they've reached an emotional plateau in their relationship with narcotics. They have extracted from them everything they could. If whatever drug they are using hasn't killed them, that is the point at which they are ready to ready to begin to disconnect.

Yet there are real ramifications to this approach. Narcotics use exacts a significant toll on your biology. As scientists will tell you, the liver, lungs, and digestive tract you are born with are the only ones you probably will get to own in this lifetime. And organs are like shoes. You pound the pavement with them daily, and the soles are bound to wear thin and offer poor protection to your feet. You need to know that while it is your body, it is also an irreplaceable gift given to you.

There is a lot of inner work that you or your family members struggling with addiction can do to make it possible for you to be ready emotionally. One way is to help your body free itself from the chemical dependence and interrupt the cycle of compulsive behavior.

The other is to raise the "bottom." It used to be that doctors and other treatment experts believed that you couldn't help anyone unless they wanted help, and that most addicts wouldn't accept help until they'd lost everything except their lives, and were close to losing those, too.

I disagree. Jail is a bottom. Losing a spouse is a bottom. Losing children is a bottom. Losing a home is a bottom. What we do at Creative care is point out the direction of where things are going, stressing that if the addict doesn't stop, these bottoms will inevitably reached. We tackle two of the cornerstones of addiction: minimizing and denial. If you can take the blinders off an addict, he can no longer justify denial.

Addicts do need a bottom, but death needn't be the only bottom.

It sounds easier said than done, but let me give you an example of what I mean. You see, we don't merely point out the obvious: we walk our patients, step by step, through how things will develop if they don't change the course of their lives. If a patient has been arrested twice for driving while intoxicated, we point out to them that they may kill someone or kill themselves next. Don't they still deny? Yes, in fact. Which is why we use another tool: we enlist family and friends and employers into the confrontation (and that's usually what it amounts to). The reason? Because the addict doesn't realize the extent of his denial, but when you use information that others have given you to control the addict, it becomes a lot harder for them to minimize. I'll tell a patient, "You said you've only done X once before; your brother says he has seen you do X on these occasions."

We also raise the bottom for our patients in group therapy—or, I should say, their peers do it for us. There's almost nothing more effective in righting an addict's path than being called out for their actions, or inactions, by another addict who knows all about self-deception. Often what you'll find is that several of the addicts will say outright, "You're wasting your time; you're not going to get sober if you continue with your behavior." When such interventions happen routinely, they have a lasting impact.

14

❧

Medication to Stop Dependence

ALTHOUGH SCIENTISTS AND ADDICTION experts have long believed that the brain chemistry of an addict differs from that of an individual who isn't addicted to alcohol or drugs, only recently have scientists been able to prove as much, using advanced brain-imaging technology.

As I mentioned earlier, today researchers have a much better understanding of how addiction can hijack the brain by turning its reward circuits against it. In some individuals, alcohol and drugs like cocaine interfere with the neurotransmitter dopamine, a key chemical messenger in the brain that helps it with everything from simple movement to feelings of enjoyment. In those cases, the drugs and/or alcohol trick the brain into producing more dopamine and worse, over time, dominates its production to the exclusion of the healthy activities that once prompted its release. More, the effects of dopamine taper off over time for those individuals, forcing them to drink more and more in order to enjoy the same happy feelings.

Scientists believe that they are getting closer to figuring out how to fix addiction, too. Operating on the principle that addiction is a physical disorder that hampers the brain's ability to process decisions, pleasure, and inhibition control in the same way that nonaddicts do, researchers and pharmaceutical companies are working on developing medications to treat addiction. Whether that promise will be realized remains to be seen, although there is no shortage of people giving it a shot. Both the National Institute on Drug Abuse and the National Institute on Alcohol Abuse and Alcoholism are currently studying or funding studies of roughly 200 addiction medications.

In addition, a number of drugs prescribed to help addicts quit, such as methadone, a synthetic opioid, help stabilize the condition of heroin and morphine addicts, which are also opioids. However, it should be cautioned that these drugs are highly addictive. A newer model is buprenorphine, approved by the Food and Drug Administration (FDA) earlier this decade. It's used for the same purpose and ostensibly causes less dependence.

For decades, alcoholics have been given Antabuse (disulfiram), which makes them sick to their stomachs if they drink alcohol. (It prevents the alcohol from being broken down in the liver, so five to ten minutes after people gulp down a drink, they experience the effects of a hangover—flushed skin, nausea, and vomiting— for anywhere from half an hour to several hours afterward.)

There's also naltrexone—sold under the brands Depade, Vivitrol, and Revia. It was originally developed to treat addiction to painkillers but approved for the treatment of alcoholism in 1994 and shown in studies cited by the U.S. Department of Health and Human Services to help some alcoholics quit or dramatically cut down on their drinking.

Newer is Vivitrol, an injectable form of naltrexone, which the FDA approved in 2006; it's given as a shot once a month.

None of the medications currently being used to treat addiction are perfect, but in recent years, scientists have made great strides in learning how addiction impacts the brain (and vice versa). Biopharmaceutical companies are eagerly cultivating a new generation of medications that I will discuss in this chapter.

MEDICATION MOTIVE

A few notes about motive. Obviously, pharmaceutical companies argue that addiction is chronic and that like other chronic diseases, such as diabetes, it needs to be treated with medicine. Universally, I don't believe that to be true, but many addicts do have emotional issues that benefit from treatment, if not require it. I know firsthand how helpful particular medications can be in stabilizing addicts, making their deeper therapeutic work more effective.

Let me preface what follows by saying that I do not always advocate medicating my patients. More, I fully appreciate why the addiction community traditionally has been wary of medication, seeing it as another drug to be avoided. After all, numerous factors render the administration of certain drugs and medical procedures completely inadvisable for some addicts.

Still, many addictive disorders cannot truly be treated without also addressing a coexisting emotional or psychiatric disorder, and often that issue requires a medical solution. Someone who is delusional or hallucinating cannot enter addiction treatment for cocaine, for example, without first being given the tools to control the delusions (which are symptomatic of psychosis and mania).

All addicts should participate in the decision to begin the use of a medication.

Naturally, they must be educated about a medication's makeup, the reasons for its use, the alternatives that are available, and the side effects that the medication is known to cause (which can be very unglamorous, indeed). And only when an individual agrees with the doctor's recommendation should a treatment course be started.

CLASSES OF MEDICATIONS

Pharmacological medications, which can alter mood, behavior, and energy levels, can be perfectly appropriate for nonaddicted people with emotional issues, but in addicts who have depression, anxiety, schizophrenic, or bipolar disorder, the risk of abuse is very high.

There are five classes of medications used to treat dual-disorder individuals. They include antiaddiction, antianxiety, antidepression, antimania, and antipsychotic medications.

Antiaddiction Medications

Antiaddiction treatments, also called small-molecule therapies, block a drug's neural targets, so that when it reaches the brain, it has nowhere to go. The medications have been around for decades, but they have been only partially successful, partly because many of them have major downsides. Most notably, methadone (sold under the brand Amidone and many users), used to treat heroin addicts, has itself been linked with addiction and overdose deaths because it actually mimics heroin, producing its own high. In fact, in 2006, the National Center of Health Statistics listed methadone as a factor in the deaths of nearly 3,000 people that year, four-fifths of which were accidental deaths and involved a combination of methadone with other drugs. Other adverse effects include constipation, nausea, and hypotension.

The antiaddiction medications that we prescribe most often are naltrexone and, to a far lesser extent, disulfiram (sold under the brand Antabuse). These can offer a short-term crutch, and they can be used in extreme situations, such as during heroin withdrawal or extreme alcoholism. Antabuse also can be used in special situations. For example, if treatment is interrupted treatment for a three-day family visit, Antabuse can help protect the addict from relapse.

At Creative Care, we have had perhaps the most success with naltrexone, which can cut down drastically on substance intake. (Many patients benefit from a period of sobriety during which they learn to stay sober without the medication.) Naltrexone is used only for finite periods, and combined with other components of treatment, such as psychotherapy. The reason: unpleasant side effects, including allergic reactions, insomnia, headaches, and impotence.

Yet another generation of antiaddiction medications is on the horizon, and researchers are working on new approaches. One is through a vaccine that would teach the body's immune system to assail a drug before it reaches the brain. (Already vaccines that turn the body's defense system against cocaine and other addictive substances, such as nicotine, methamphetamines, and heroin, are in development.)

The concept of "inoculating" those at risk of addiction is attracting attention, too, because it just may work, and because the idea of a vaccine, long associated with treating infectious diseases, helps underscore that alcoholism is not a moral failing but a physical condition with an emotional undercurrent. It's also less scary sounding than treating addicts with "drugs."

The strides being made are very encouraging. In the meantime, we prescribe antiaddiction medications only to addicts who have relapsed more than once and are clearly losing the struggle against their addiction. Even then, we constantly evaluate them.

Antianxiety Medications

As with chronic conditions such as heart disease, emotional issues are astonishingly complex, and probably result from a combination of environmental, psychological, developmental, and genetic factors. How and why they come together in a way that causes some people to suffer more than others is still being examined, though. For example, scientists still do not fully understand why some people are sent over the edge by a trauma while others who have experienced the same trauma will more easily move forward in their lives.

Scientists are beginning to get a handle on anxiety disorders, which differ from normal anxiety in that they can be crippling. Afflicted individuals experience acute feelings of dread that overwhelm the situation (say, when they have to give a speech), and likely they will shake, sweat, become flush, and experience heart palpitations. The anxiety is troubling for the afflicted individual, and it can make everyday nervousness feel like a walk in the park.

The two parts of the brain that researchers believe are most responsible for anxiety disorders are the hippocampus and the amygdala. The hippocampus, in the temporal lobe, is made up of two hippocampi, one on each side of the brain, and they are responsible for spatial relations and long-term memory. The hippocampus is also the part of the brain that transforms threatening experiences into memories.

Interestingly, studies have shown that the hippocampus appears slightly smaller in individuals who were abused as children,[1] although researchers are still determining what causes its reduced size and what role that reduction plays in how people play back their memories as well as in anxiety disorders. (What researchers and neuroscientists can agree on is that the hippocampus has an essential role in the way that new memories about past events are formed.)

The small, almond-shaped amygdala—which has long been linked with emotions and fears—rests a few inches from either ear in the temporal lobe, not far from the hippocampus. It can alert the rest of the brain when a threat is present, triggering fear or anxiety. Indeed, a web of nerves surges through the amygdala, connecting it to several other important parts of the brain, including the visual cortex and the neocortex—circuits that researchers are beginning to think might be even more crucial than the amygdala itself.

As scientists learn more and more about how our brains make us experience fear and anxiety, they may target specific neurotransmitters and develop drugs to block those neurotransmitters and assuage extreme responses.

In the meantime, the medications that are mainly used in anxiety disorders are tranquilizers called benzodiazepines, or "benzos." Benzos cannot cure a person's anxiety disorder, but they can keep the anxiety under control while he or she undergoes psychotherapy.

Benzos do have side effects. A minor side effect is drowsiness. A much bigger issue is that they are potentially addictive. Indeed, typically they are prescribed only for short periods; the longer they are taken, the more benzos are needed to experience the same result. (Particularly because addicts become dependent on medications so quickly, they must be monitored closely while on benzos, and the course of treatment must be very short.)

Some of the most widely described benzos are clonazepam, lorazepam, and alprazolam, each better known by the brand names under which they are sold: Klonopin, Ativan, and Xanax. All are useful for general anxiety disorder, and use of each should be tapered off systematically and slowly. (Withdrawal symptoms and anxiety can surface if the medication is stopped too abruptly.)

Because benzos can be problematic for some people, a newer class of antianxiety medication has surfaced in the last 20 years called azapirones—better known by their brand names, the most widely recognized of which is BuSpar. Azapirones have no signs of being potentially addictive; neither do they make users drowsy—two big pluses. One small concern worth noting is that they need to be taken *precisely as prescribed* to be effective and to minimize their side effects, including dizziness and nausea. Meanwhile, benzos can be taken from once to three times a day or simply on an as-needed basis.

Last, there are beta-blockers, which are first and foremost blood pressure drugs but are also sometimes prescribed to dampen the physical symptoms of anxiety disorders. One of the most popular beta-blockers is propranolol, known better under its brand name of Inderal. Inderal is used to treat chest pain, tremors, heart rhythm disorders and other heart conditions, and to cut down on the frequency and severity of migraine headaches. But doctors prescribe beta-blockers for a wide array of issues, as they prevent the physical symptoms that accompany certain anxiety disorders, particularly social phobia. (They're very useful in situations where someone knows of an upcoming, highly stressful situation, such as when he or she has to give a toast or receive an award before a roomful of people.)

Antidepressants

With antidepressant medications so common—according to estimates, 8 to 9 percent of Americans take them, including

20 percent of all adult American women—critics wonder whether they're being overprescribed and if they're causing people to lose their ability to cope (or the rationale for trying).

I still remember reading, and enjoying, an article in *Time* magazine titled "When Sadness Is a Good Thing."[2] The author of the piece, John Cloud, based his argument—that we as a society have turned the blues into a disorder—in part on a book by college professors Allan Horwitz and Jerome Wakefield called *The Loss of Sadness: How Psychiatry Transformed Normal Sorrow into Depressive Disorder*. In it, Horowitz and Wakefield explain that loss responses are part of our biological heritage as human beings. Cloud goes on to elaborate:

> Nonhuman primates separated from sexual partners or peers have physiological responses that correlate with sadness, including higher levels of certain hormones. Human infants express despair to evoke sympathy from others. These sadness responses suggest sorrow is genetic and that it is useful for attracting social support, protecting us from aggressors and teaching us that whatever prompted the sadness—say, getting fired because you were always late to work—is behavior to be avoided. This is a brutal economic approach to the mind, but it makes sense: we are sometimes meant to suffer emotional pain so that we will make better choices.

I couldn't agree more with Cloud—as well as Horowitz and Wakefield—that over the last couple of decades, antidepressants have come to be dispensed with all the economy of candy on Halloween night. I also worry that, like the very concept of addiction treatment—which has been hijacked by recreational "rehab" caregivers and turned into a bit of a punch line in the popular culture—depression will come to be taken less seriously as a result.

That would be a shame, because while alarmingly high numbers of people are medicated now who needn't and shouldn't be, there are plenty of legitimately depressed individuals who cannot simply flip a switch that energizes them or jump-starts their brains. And for those people, medication is a far better solution than other alternatives, including self-injury and even suicide.

Indeed, while antidepressents shouldn't be doled out like M&Ms, consider this: Oncologists do not treat their cancer patients by telling them to keep a stiff upper lip. Diabetologists do not treat their diabetic patients with encouraging words, either. Psychiatrists and other clinicians do not treat their clinically depressed patients with advice to snap out of it. And as long as a clinically depressed individual isn't coerced into medication, I am a firm believer in giving them the tools available to help them get better.

So, how long are antidepressants taken, and what is their impact? First, antidepressants do not cure depression. What they can do is help an addict with moderate to severe depression go into remission, which, along with psychotherapy, is the best path toward becoming a healthy individual over the long term.

It's not an overnight process, nor is it an eternal one. Most antidepressants begin altering an individual's brain chemistry with the first dose, but it takes between four to six weeks for the symptoms of depression to more fully dissipate.

Some of the newest antidepressants are called selective serotonin reuptake inhibitors (SSRIs), the most popular ones being Prozac, Zoloft, and Paxil. They work by slowing the brain's absorption of serotonin, a neurotransmitter I've mentioned before that helps control mood and promotes feelings of well-being. Serotonin is attracted to receptors within the brain, and those receptors contain enzymes that break the serotonin down. SSRIs slow the action of those enzymes so that they can't do their job effectively, and the person taking the SSRI enjoys a surge in serotonin level.

Very similarly, a lack of dopamine—another key chemical messenger in the brain that helps with a wide array of functions, including feelings of enjoyment—can contribute to depression. As a result, many of today's antidepressants work to promote the brain's supply of dopamine, including bupropion—better known by its brand name, Wellbutrin.

Meanwhile, venlafaxine, sold under the brand name Effexor, works in completely opposite fashion: It stalls the brain's absorption of both neurotransmitters. (Effexor is also commonly prescribed to treat general anxiety disorder.)

In my experience, many patients respond better to SSRIs than to atypical antidepressants, such as Wellbutrin. But both have undesirable side effects, including sexual dysfunction, insomnia, and nervousness.

Yet another class of antidepressants predates both atypical antidepressants and SSRIs: the tricyclics, named after their three-ringed molecular structure.

Tricyclics, introduced in the 1950s, were the first choice of doctors for a long time. Today they have largely been displaced by SSRIs, but they are effective in treating clinical depression as well as migraine headaches, insomnia, and a number of other conditions. (The biggest downside with tricyclics is that people often experience their side effects—dry mouth, constipation, weight gain, and blurry vision—*before* their symptoms of the depression begin to dissipate, exacerbating their poor state of mind. The biggest upside is that they work and they aren't addictive.)

But tricyclics weren't the first antidepression medications. They, too, have forebears, called monoamine oxidase inhibitors (MAOIs), which are the oldest class of antidepressant medications. MAOIs work, especially when it comes to individuals with atypical depression, a condition in which even depressed individuals can respond happily to happy events. (In contrast, those with major depression enjoy no mood swings but rather remain in a dark mood regardless of circumstances.)

Unfortunately, MAOIs dramatically limit everything else a taker can ingest, from wine, to cheese, to many over-the-counter medications. Because of this fact, they have become little more than a doctor's last line of defense.

Antimania Medications

Antimania drugs are used primarily to treat the manic phase of bipolar disorder. Most people being treated for bipolar disorder are given lithium, which has been around forever (it was the first mood-stabilizing drug approved by the FDA for children ages 12 and older), and is still the most effective mood-stabilizing medication for controlling mania and preventing the recurrence of both depressive and manic episodes.

But sometimes additional meds are prescribed for shorter periods, as when someone is enduring an episode of mania or depression that overwhelms the mood stabilizer. For example, valproates can be very useful for hard-to-treat bipolar episodes. Valproates are chemical compounds that are also used as anticonvulsants and treat a wide variety of conditions, including epilepsy, migraine headaches, and schizophrenia, in addition to bipolar disorder.

Depakote, a brand of valproic acid, is a popular anticonvulsant medication that was first approved by the FDA in 1983 for epilepsy and approved 12 years later to treat the manic episodes associated with bipolar disorder. It works by boosting an inhibitory transmitter called gamma-aminobutyric acid (GABA), a chemical that carries messages between brain nerve cells. GABA suppresses the transmission of certain nerve signals, which is critical in order to rapidly stabilize acute mania.

Geodon, meanwhile, the trade name for ziprasidone, is really an antipsychotic medication used to treat both schizophrenics and those with bipolar disorder—who can, in extreme cases, also suffer from hallucinations. It's much newer, having been approved by the FDA in 2001.

All the antimania drugs do have a downside, including undesirable side effects, such as weight gain, nausea, decreased sexual drive, anxiety, hair loss, tremors, and/or dry mouth.

The good news is that a change in the prescribed dosage can relieve all of these things. (The same is true of most of the medications listed in this chapter.)

More, the medications can be life-saving, because they protect individuals with bipolar disorder from rapid and dangerous cycling between high and low episodes.

ANTIPSYCHOTIC MEDICATIONS

Like tricyclics, antipsychotic drugs first became available in the 1950s. They have done wonders for many individuals suffering the symptoms of schizophrenia, too, although unfortunately, no antipsychotic medication can cure or insure against future episodes. (I also say antipsychotic drugs help "many" rather than "all" schizophrenics, because unfortunately not every individual with schizophrenia responds to medication.)

But the newest antipsychotic drugs—called atypical antipsychotics and introduced in the 1990s—include olanzapine, quetiapine, aripiprazole, and risperidone, known better by the most widely prescribed brands under which they are prescribed: Zyprexa, Seroquel, Abilify, and Risperdal, respectively.

All are very effective in treating hallucinations and delusions but not as effective when it comes to emotional outbursts and loss of motivation, two lesser-known hallmarks of schizophrenia. (Indeed, occasionally individuals afflicted with schizophrenia are also prescribed antidepressants to combat the intensified depression they may experience because of the antipsychotics they take.)

Clozapine, sold as Clorzaril, is perhaps the most effective of the atypical antipsychotics, although occasionally its side effects are even more severe than depressions. To wit, clozapine can fuel a condition wherein an individual loses the white blood cells that fight infection; for this reason, those who take the drug must take blood tests every other week to ensure that their white blood cell count remains stable.[3]

The silver lining in antipsychotics are that the drugs are not addictive, nor do they hijack the thought process. Although antipsychotics can cause some drowsiness, they are not designed to whitewash a person's personality or to anesthetize a person's essence but strictly to lessen the agitation, confusion, and the delusions of a psychotic episode—in other words, to help someone with schizophrenia navigate the world more lucidly.

LIMITS OF MEDICATION

I cannot emphasize enough that when we prescribe medication, it's in concert with a much broader, sophisticated treatment program. Specifically, no medicine is effective for someone suffering from both an emotional issue and a substance abuse issue unless it is complemented by active psychotherapy.

The inescapable fact is that medication can be dangerous—even deadly—when it is given to someone who cannot handle it.

That is why it is exceedingly important for psychiatrists or other clinicians to know when they are treating an addict and for them to understand how medications interact with addictions. Some drugs have side effects that might provoke relapse. Some can be lethal in combination with alcohol or certain street drugs. For this reason, it is *imperative* that the individual be honest, about everything, and that doctors take extra precautions to ensure the veracity of what they are being told.

I do not advocate treating every addict with medication. I do, however, strongly believe in the inarguable benefits of many medications for those who need them, particularly the many non-narcotic, nonaddictive medications that have emerged in the last 5 to 15 years.

Moving Forward

M Y DEEPEST WISH IS that in reading this book, you have come to understand one of the most pervasive—and best-hidden—plagues in our society today. I'm not talking about addicts; I'm talking about ignorance regarding addiction.

The sad fact is that of the roughly 12,000 treatment centers in the United States, only a tiny handful makes any attempt to treat addiction as an issue with a major emotional component when, in fact, people suffering from both are all around us.

People in trouble are simply not getting the help they need, either. Most programs center on the 12 Steps, supplementing them with group therapy and drug and alcohol education. But for many addicts, self-examination in meetings and with a sponsor is not enough. Most addicts have issues that require much more than a sympathetic listener and community support. They need therapy and, sometimes, medication. If emotional and psychiatric issues are not properly treated, addicts are doomed to relapse. Even if they succeed in quitting, they'll discover that, in sobriety, they still have to face their old demons: depression, anxiety, or whatever their issues may be. And eventually, their problems will drive them back to drugs or drink.

As you've read in these pages, some addicts do seek treatment for their emotional issues, and in so doing they are confronted with obstacle after obstacle. It frustrates me to no end that individuals seeking treatment for an emotional issue must often forgo or compromise treatment for their addiction, in part because many mental health professionals wrongly believe that if they tackle the issues underlying addiction, the habit will clear up all by itself. Worse, insurance companies help maintain this division. It is very rare for them to cover both forms of care, and even when they cover substance abuse treatment, the benefits they offer are extremely limited. (It's even harder to convince insurance companies to cover psychiatric treatment.)

DOING OUR PART

We, as a society, need to do our part. Being more aware of some of the antiquated misconceptions to which we cling—such as that emotional and psychiatric issues are not legitimate medical problems and that you can "get over" such issues if you really try—is one piece of it. The fact remains that as hard as it is for someone to admit to a substance abuse problem, it's even harder for a person to admit to struggling with what is popularly referred to as "mental illness"—that is, emotional and psychiatric issues, because of those wrong ideas.

Really encouraging change on an institutional level may be even more vital, whether it is through letter writing, petitions, calling your local politicians, or speaking with local media about the issue.

If we can impact our healthcare system so that far greater coop-eration can and will exist between the fields of addiction treatment and mental health, we will have come a long way in saving lives.

It's not beyond reach. Progress is being made, every year. Already some states have done away with separate mental health and addiction agencies, so that their residents' insurance now pro-vides for the integrated treatment of both their addiction and emotional issues.

And despite the many shortcomings by medical insurers when it comes to addiction treatment—many simply do not cover it—progress is being made, albeit slowly. Most states at this point require some group health insurance to cover treatment for alco-hol and other drug addictions. (Seven do not, including Arizona, Iowa, Oklahoma, and Wyoming. The Web site www.natlalliance. org outlines what each state mandates.)

Further, every state has an agency that plans and administers addiction treatment services and that has limited funding for those without insurance or with too little insurance. Medicare and state Medicaid plans also provide some limited treatment services for those who are eligible.

Part of the shift toward insurance parity reform—in other words, requiring that emotional and psychiatric issues be treated in exactly the same way as physical illness—is due to the growing body of evidence that treatment works. One of the biggest hur-dles to insurance reform was the widespread belief that addiction treatment is ineffective; now numerous studies show that 30 to 60 percent of individuals who enter treatment programs stay absti-nent for one year or longer.

More, today there is less emphasis on permanent abstinence as the exclusive measure of treatment effectiveness. The reality is that alcoholism, like diabetes and many cancers, is a chronic disorder, and complete recovery after a single treatment is, as with diabetes and many cancers, extremely rare.

Indeed, a more educated population is already beginning to appreciate that success can mean dramatically decreased substance abuse as well as long periods of abstinence. By this measure, success rates are far higher. Hazelden, for example, which refers many patients to Creative Care for further treatment, submits that three-quarters of its patients are abstinent at the end of one year, a figure that includes both those who've managed complete abstinence as well as those who've fallen off the wagon once in that period and gotten back on it.

Also important are studies showing that while certainly helpful to countless numbers of people, Alcoholics Anonymous is not a panacea. In fact, in 2006, one controlled study of roughly 3,500 men and women concluded that AA and other 12-step programs are in no way superior to any other intervention in reducing alcohol dependence or alcohol-related problems.[1]

MORE STUDIES, CONCRETE RESULTS

Today more attention is being paid to the toll of not treating those who are unwell, in wide-ranging studies on everything from crime rates as some individuals wind up on the streets, to hospitalizations, to jail, to fatalities, to the economic costs to the country, which many estimates peg at between $200 billion and $300 billion annually. (According to a 1996 study by the Bureau of National Affairs, an independent publisher of information, such estimates include $500 million in lost workdays; premature employee deaths, including from on-the-job accidents; and health treatment costs. The study found that substance abusers also file five times the number of workers' compensation claims as do nonaddicts.)

And more scientists are rallying behind the need for anyone with both an emotional issue and an addiction—not just those lucky few with enough money to pay for private insurance—to be referred to a residential treatment program that provides integrated co-occurring treatment, such as the kind we offer at Creative Care.

Because the overhead at such facilities is different—staff members must be able to address both mental health and addiction—costs for such treatment will always be higher up front than at traditional programs that focus on one or the other. But in the long run, such treatment will save the healthcare system billions of dollars by improving the well-being of individuals who would deteriorate otherwise.

A 2001 study by the University of California San Francisco and Kaiser Permanente came to the same conclusion.[2] For the study, researchers looked at the differences in treatment outcomes between integrated and independent models of medical care and substance abuse treatment. Their conclusion? People benefit more from integrated treatment, and, over time, integrated treatment is more cost-effective. In fact, the study strongly suggested that keeping medical care and substance abuse services separate and uncoordinated is ludicrous because so many medical conditions are related to the substance abuse, including chronic liver disease, hepatitis C, and psychiatric conditions including depression and anxiety.

The two-year study involved nearly 600 men and women who were admitted to the Kaiser Permanente Chemical Dependency Recovery Program in Sacramento. The subjects were randomly assigned to receive treatment either through an integrated model or an independent treatment model where primary care and addiction treatment were provided separately.

Nearly all of the study subjects showed progress in tackling their addictions (to alcohol, amphetamines, marijuana, cocaine, and sedatives). But 69 percent of those individuals with addiction-related illnesses—both medical and psychiatric—were more likely to be abstinent in the integrated care group than in the independent care group, where just 55 percent were able to remain abstinent. That 14 percent difference is very significant, and it's something the insurance industry is taking note of.

More good news is that doctors are also beginning to better understand the effectiveness of working with other doctors to provide treatment for both mental health and addiction in a coordinated way. Through education and better training, they're coming to appreciate that unless interventions are bundled, people don't receive the consistent and seamless treatment they need. By approaching emotional and addiction issues simultaneously and in close concert, caregivers can gain a far better picture of someone's needs and how they can work together to address them.

Much of what's left to do is to simply educate people in the field. As the grassroots mental health organization National Alliance on Mental Illness stresses to its members and community leaders, people working in recovery need to realize finally that substance abuse counseling and traditional mental health counseling are *different approaches* that must be *reconciled* to treat co-occurring disorders. It's important for them to know, for example, that it isn't enough for a person with bipolar disorder to be taught relationship skills; it's also important to explore how the person can avoid relationships that are intertwined with his or her substance abuse.

It's also important for all of us who are touched by addiction to understand a person's limitations when it comes to integrated treatment. While you might hear that someone must be clean and sober before their emotional issues can be addressed, I hope that by now you understand that abstinence can't always be a condition for receiving treatment, since not all patients understand the severity of their issues, both the addiction and the emotional ones. And almost always, denial is a key part of the overall problem. (We saw this most clearly in the case of Elizabeth, whom you met earlier in the book.)

UNTIL NEXT TIME

I hope that, in these pages, I've helped you to understand why the way to vanquish addiction is to tackle the emotional issues behind it. I also hope that the stories of some of Creative Care's former patients have shown why there is every reason to believe that working through both the emotional and addiction issues is possible and can be life-changing. I hope they've shown why there is absolutely no reason to abandon hope and how, when given the right tool set, any addict can become well.

The path to recovery is never an easy one. Often there are setbacks. At times the cycle can seem relentless and unbreakable. But there is truth to the old adage that it is darkest before the dawn. People on the verge of throwing their lives away for reasons others may not understand *can* be pulled from the brink and *do* go on to live happy, fulfilling, giving, sober lives. The first step toward that future is better understanding.

For 25 years, my wonderful staff and I have been able to help addicts by tackling both the physical and the emotional roots of addiction. I hope this window into our world, and into the lives of the people who have helped shape our own, has helped you, too.

Notes

CHAPTER 2

1. J. Noble, *Textbook of Primary Care Medicine*, 3rd ed. (St. Louis, Mo: Mosby, 2001).
2. National Survey on Drug Use & Health, SAMHSA, 2005, http://www.oas.samhsa.gov/nsduh.htm.
3. Ibid.
4. Ernest Kurtz, *Alcoholics Anonymous and the Disease Concept of Alcoholism*, http://www.bhrm.org/papers/AAand DiseaseConcept.pdf
5. Results from University of Indiana study cited in *Alcoholism: Clinical & Experimental Research* (May 2006).
6. Results from San Diego State University cited in *Alcoholism: Clinical & Experimental Research* (August 2007).

CHAPTER 4

1. The National Council on Alcoholism and Drug Dependence: 244 East 58th Street, 4th Floor, New York, NY 10022. Phone: (212) 269-7797. Fax: 212/269-7510. Email: national@ ncadd.org. Website: http://www.ncadd.org. HOPE LINE: (800) NCA-CALL (24-hour affiliate referral).
2. Research conducted by the Hazeldon Foundation for the Home Box Office show *Addiction*: "Workplace Addiction Survey" of 200 U.S. companies, from Fortune 500 firms to small businesses.

3.   HealthStyles Survey, licensed from Porter Novelli by SAMHSA and the Centers for Disease Control and Prevention, 2006 (released November 27).

4.   Stanley D. Rosenberg, Ph.D., Robert E. Drake, M.D., Ph.D., George L. Wolford, Ph.D., Kim T. Mueser, Ph.D., Thomas E. Oxman, M.D., Robert M. Vidaver, M.D., Karen L. Carrieri, R.N., M.A., and Ravindra Luckoor, M.D., "Dartmouth Assessment of Lifestyle Instrument (DALI): A Substance Use Disorder Screen for People With Severe Mental Illness," *American Journal of Psychiatry* 155 (1998): 232–235. See website http://dms.dartmouth.edu/prc/instruments/DALI.pdf.

5.   *The Diagnostic and Statistical Manual of Mental Disorders*, published by the American Psychiatric Association, is a handbook for mental health professionals that lists categories of conditions and the criteria for diagnosing them.

CHAPTER 5

1.   Center for Substance Abuse, "Substance Abuse Treatment for Persons with Child Abuse and Neglect Issues: Treatment Improvement Protocol Series No. 36." DDHS Publication No. (SMA) 00-3357 (Washington, DC: U.S. Government Printing Office, 2000).

CHAPTER 6

1.   R. W. Pickens, D. S. Svikis, M. McGue, D. T. Lykken, L. L. Heston, and P. J. Clayton, "Heterogeneity in the inheritance of alcoholism," *Archives of General Psychiatry* 48 (1991): 19–28.

2.   Sir Michael Rutter, and David J. Smith, *Psycho-social Disorders in Young People* (New York: John Wiley & Sons, 1995).

3. Study published by the National Institute on Alcohol Abuse and Alcoholism, part of the National Institutes of Health, in February 2007 and reproduced in article form: Jodi M. Gilman, James M. Bjork, and Daniel W. Hommer, "Parental Alcohol Use and Brain Volumes in Early- and Late-Onset Alcoholics," *Biological Psychiatry* 62, 6 (September 15, 2007): 607–615.

4. J. D. Grant, A. C. Heath, K. K. Bucholz., P. A. F. Madden, A. Agrawal, D. J. Stratham, N. G. Martin. *Alcoholism: Clinical & Experimental Research* 31, 5 (May 2007): 717–728.

5. Information from the American Psychological Association fact sheet, "Understanding Alcohol Use Disorders and Their Treatment." Contributors include Peter E. Nathan, Ph.D.; John Wallace, Ph.D.; Joan Zweben, Ph.D.; and A. Thomas Horvath, Ph.D.

6. Study results by Willemien Langeland and Onno van der Hart published in the journal *Alcoholism: Clinical & Experimental Research* (March 2004).

CHAPTER 7

1. Study conducted by Michael D. De Bellis, professor of psychiatry and behavioral sciences and director of the Healthy Childhood Brain Development Research Program at Duke University Medical Center. *Alcoholism: Clinical & Experimental Research* (September 2005).

2. Gary S. Wand, *Alcoholism: Clinical & Experimental Research* 26, 11 (November 2002): 1625–1631.

3. E. P. Noble, S. M. Berman, T. Z. Ozkaragoz, and T. Ritchie, "Prolonged P300 latency in children with the D2 dopamine receptor A1 allele," *American Journal of Human Genetics*, April 1994., pages 658–668.

CHAPTER 8

1. J. M. Polich, D. J. Armor, and H. B. Braiker, "Stability and Change in Drinking Patterns," in *The Course of Alcoholism: Four Years After Treatment* (New York: John Wiley & Sons, 1981), pp. 159–200; W. A. Hunt, L. W. Barnett, and L. G. Branch, "Relapse Rates in Addictions Programs," *Journal of Clinical Psychology* 27: 455–456, 1971.

2. Findings by the nation's medical research agency, the National Institutes of Health, which is part of the U.S. Department of Health and Human Services.

3. Ibid.

4. Joseph Volpicelli, M.D., Ph.D., Geetha Balaraman, Julie Hahn, Heather Wallace, M.A., and Donald Bux, Ph.D., *Alcohol Research & Health* 23, 4 (1999): 256–262.

5. Volpicelli et al., *Alcohol Research & Health* 23: 256–262.

6. S. E. Hyman, "Genetics and Etiology of Schizophrenia and Bipolar Disorder," *Biological Psychiatry* 47, 3: 171–173.

7. R. C. Kessler et al., "Prevalence, Severity, and Comorbidity of Twelve-Month DSM-IV Disorders in the National Comorbidity Survey Replication (NCS-R)," *Archives of General Psychiatry* 62, 6 (June 2005): 617–627.

8. James H. Meador-Woodruff, Alan J. Hogg, Jr. and Robert E. Smith of the Mental Health Research Institute and Department of Psychiatry, University of Michigan, *Brain Research Bulletin* 55, 5 (July 15, 2001): 631–640.

9. N. A. Huxley, S. V. Parikh, and R. J. Baldessarini, "Effectiveness of Psychosocial Treatments in Bipolar Disorder: State of the Evidence," *Harvard Review of Psychiatry* 8, 3 (2000): 126–40.

10. Led by Yih-Ing Hser, Ph.D., of the University of California, Los Angeles. Heroin addicts were admitted to the California Civil Addict Program between 1962 and 1964.

CHAPTER 9

1. A.A. Fact File, Prepared by General Service Office of Alcoholics Anonymous, 2007.

2. G.K. Brown et al., "Cognitive Therapy for the Prevention of Suicide Attempts: A Randomized Controlled Trial," *Journal of the American Medical Association* 294, 5 (2005): 563–570.

3. G.S. Sachs and M.E. Thase, "Bipolar Disorder Therapeutics: Maintenance Treatment," *Biological Psychiatry* 48, 6 (2000): 573–581.

4. Kathleen M. Carroll, Bruce J. Rounsaville, and Daniel S. Keller, "Relapse Prevention Strategies for the Treatment of Cocaine Abuse," *American Journal of Drug and Alcohol Abuse* 17, 3 (1991): 249–265.

5. Mark P. McGovern, Ph.D., Bonnie R. Wrisley, B.A. and Robert E. Drake, Ph.D., "Relapse of Substance Use Disorder and Its Prevention Among Persons With Co-occurring Disorders," *Psychiatric Services* 56 (October 2005): 1270–1273.

6. Chutuape, Silverman, and Stitzer, "Use of Methadone Take-Home Contingencies with Persistent Opiate and Cocaine Abusers," *Journal of Substance Abuse Treatment* 16, 1 (1998): 23–30; Sigmon, Steingard, Badger, Anthony & Higgins, "Voucher-based Contingent Reinforcement of Marijuana Abstinence among Individuals with Serious Mental Illness," *Journal of Substance Abuse Treatment* 30, 4 (2000): 291–295.

CHAPTER 11

1. J. D. Bodkin, G. L. Zornberg, S. E. Lukas, J. O. Cole, "Buprenorphine treatment of refractory depression," *Journal of Clinical Psychopharmacology* 15,1 (February 1995): 49–57.

CHAPTER 13

1. R. C. Kessler, W. T. Chiu, O. Demler, E. E. Walters, "Prevalence, severity, and comorbidity of twelve-month DSM-IV disorders in the National Comorbidity Survey Replication (NCS-R)," *Archives of General Psychiatry* 62, 6 (June 2005): 617–627.
2. Barkur S. Shastsry, "Bipolar Disorder: An Update," *Neurochemistry International* 46, 4 (March 2005): 273–279.
3. Ibid.

CHAPTER 14

1. J. D. Bremner et al., "MRI-based Measurement of Hippocampal Volume in Combat-Related Posttraumatic Stress Disorder," *American Journal of Psychiatry* 152 (1995): 973–981.
2. John Cloud, "When Sadness Is a Good Thing," *Time*, August 16, 2007.
3. National Institutes of Mental Health.

EPILOGUE

1. Study results published in July 2006 by the Italian Agency for Public Health in Rome.
2. Coauthors of the study included researchers from the Kaiser Permanente Medical Center, Northern Region Oakland, and from Kaiser Permanente Chemical Dependency Recovery Program, Sacramento, California. Research was supported by a grant from the National Institute on Drug Abuse.

Index

INDEX

233

therapeutic massage, 133–134
therapy
  cognitive therapy, 124–128
  community reinforcement approach
      (CRA), 125–126, 130
  equine-assisted therapy, 30, 131–133
  eye movement desensitization and
      reprocessing (EMDR), 131
  facing yourself through, 121–135
  group, 29, 30, 46, 47, 78, 146, 148,
      193, 211
  individual, 29, 34, 176
  motivational enhancement training
      (MET), 126–127
  power of daily, 47
  psychoanalysis, 7, 122, 124
  psychotherapy. see psychotherapy
  relapse prevention therapy (RPT),
      128–130
  supplemental, 134–135
  therapeutic massage, 133–134
Time magazine, 203
traditional addiction treatment. see under
    treatment
trauma. see emotional trauma(s)
treatment
  and abstinence. see abstinence
  active treatment vs. sustaining
      rehabilitation, 67, 128
  adaptation, 66
  facilities/foundations. see specific facility
      names
  failure of, 4, 15, 22
  integrated vs. independent models
      of, 215–217
  and outpatient vs. inpatient care,
      143, 146, 147, 167
  outset of treatment vs. active
      treatment, 67
  recognizing addictive behavior prior
      to, 49–68
  redefining, 17–36

and relapse. see relapse
staff in, 68
traditional, 4, 19, 197, 215–216
time, in relation to trust, 68
see also therapy
tricyclics, 205, 207
trust, 68

understanding the prognosis, 65–66
uninsured Americans, 20
unprocessed trauma, 69, 70, 72, 80
U.S. Air Force, 45
U.S. Department of Health and Human
    Services, 28, 58, 85, 196
U.S. Food and Drug Administration
    (FDA), 114, 189, 196, 206–207

valproates/valproic acid, 115, 189–190,
    206
venlafaxine, 205
Vicodin, 44, 143
Vietnam veterans, 106–107
Vigabatrin, 97
Vistaril, 148
Vivitrol, 79, 196

waiting too long, to seek treatment,
    177–193
Wakefield, Jerome, 203
weakness. see personal weakness, and
    addiction
Wellbutrin, 147, 205
"When Sadness Is a Good Thing,"
    203
witnessing physical or emotional
    violence or sexual abuse, 70
writing and art therapy, 30

Xanax, 12, 45, 143, 202

ziprasidone, 189, 207
Zoloft, 204